Mary Berry is known to mil[...] [...]
networked Thames Television [...]
regular contributor to BBC *Woman's Hour* and often takes
part in BBC and local radio phone-in programmes.

Mary Berry was, for several years, cookery editor of *Ideal Home* and is now a regular contributor to *Family Circle*. She is one of Britain's most popular cookery writers and has written over twenty books. Recent publications include *Fast Cakes*, *More Fast Cakes*, *Fast Suppers*, *Fast Starters*, *Soups and Salads*, *Fast Desserts*, *Fruit Fare*, *Mary Berry's New Freezer Cookbook*, *Mary Berry's Kitchen Wisdom*, *Feed Your Family The Healthier Way* and *Buffets*.

By the same author

Fast Cakes
More Fast Cakes
Fast Suppers
Fast Starters
Soups and Salads
Fast Desserts
Fruit Fare
Mary Berry's New Freezer Cookbook
Mary Berry's Kitchen Wisdom
Feed Your Family The Healthier Way
Buffets

MARY BERRY'S

Favourite Microwave Recipes

GRAFTON BOOKS

A Division of the Collins Publishing Group

LONDON GLASGOW
TORONTO SYDNEY AUCKLAND

Grafton Books
A Division of the Collins Publishing Group
8 Grafton Street, London W1X 3LA

Published by Grafton Books 1988

First published in Great Britain by
Judy Piatkus (Publishers) Ltd 1987

ISBN 0-586-20262-5

Printed and bound in Great Britain by
Collins, Glasgow

Set in Century Schoolbook

Author's Acknowledgements

I would particularly like to thank Debbie Woolhead for her
assistance in developing and testing these recipes. We've
often found that two heads are better than one!
   I would also like to thank my family for trying out the
dishes, and giving me their valuable advice and the food their
wholehearted approval.

Contents

Acknowledgements

The author and publishers would like to thank the following for kindly allowing their colour photographs to be used in this book: Billington's Unrefined Sugars (Dry Crunchy Muesli, Soft Fruit Flan, Chilled Blackcurrant Creams, Blackberry Mousse and the Chutneys); The British Chicken Information Service (Chicken and Coconut Curry); British Meat (Fruity Pork Casserole); Cadbury Ltd (Butterscotch Fudge Cake); The Pasta Information Service (Tagliatelle al Tonno) and the Scottish Salmon Bureau (Poached Salmon with a strawberry and cucumber salad).

Introduction

I must admit that at first, I was not at all enthusiastic about cooking by microwaves. For one thing, I had always managed perfectly well without a microwave cooker and the family had always enjoyed their meals, and for another, I had heard tell of people who had rushed out and bought one, only to find that all they could manage successfully was to reheat a cup of coffee. Their attempts at actually cooking anything were doomed, it seemed. However, the more I thought about it, the more I decided that I must see for myself what the advantages and disadvantages of this 'new' cooking appliance were. So we have one. We have experimented with it, grown to appreciate it, and now it has its rightful place in the kitchen – just as my food processor has, or the set of sharp knives I find indispensable for preparing food.

The family still prefer a traditional roast and *I* prefer to cook my pasta in the usual way – on top of the conventional hob. For me, the microwave will never replace my cooker or my grill, but I have learnt to use all three in conjunction, getting the best out of each. It's a natural partner for the freezer, too, as it defrosts most things far quicker than if they were left to stand, and reheats cooked food without losing any of the fresh, full flavour.

Vegetables from the garden are a treat; mince is a particular triumph and sauces have never been so easy – but I wouldn't use the microwave for everything. We've had our share of setbacks, but gradually, I have adapted some of my favourite recipes to cook by microwave. In this book, I have included only recipes and ideas which I find really satisfactory, and I hope you will enjoy them too. The recipes are uncomplicated, easy and quick to make.

So take the plunge, try them out and soon you will also enjoy the benefits of this 'new' cooking method.

Mary Berry

Cooking With a Microwave

As you probably know, cooking by microwaves is not at all the same as cooking in the conventional way. A microwave is a short-lived, high-frequency electro-magnetic wave similar to the ones which are used for transmitting radar signals. It heats up food by penetrating it to a depth of up to an inch and a half (4 cm) and activating the molecules of water and fat and sugar, making them vibrate at millions of times a second. This produces heat by friction (as you do when you rub your hands together) and this heat travels in towards the centre of the food by conduction, passing from particle to particle, until the centre is reached.

The greatest problem with microwaving is judging the timing correctly, and the usual tendency for new microwave cooks is to *overcook* the food. Since it is usually quicker to cook this way – especially when dealing with small portions – and the heat generated on the outside of the food is so fierce it travels to the centre fast – you have to remember to remove the food from the cooker and let it finish cooking by leaving it for a brief period of *standing time* before it is ready to serve. The food – meat, fish, vegetables, a cake – will always continue to cook for a while once it is out of the microwave. So standing time is usually essential – and very useful, since you can plan your time to cook a second dish, or set the table, while the main dish is standing.

I find one main advantage is its speed, especially when the microwave is used in conjunction with my grill; maybe I need to reheat a simple Shepherd's Pie quickly for a family meal. As soon as I come in, I put the pie in the microwave to reheat, and at the same time I turn the grill on full. In 10 minutes, the potato-topped pie is reheated and I then transfer it to brown under the grill. While it is browning nicely, I cook freshly shredded cabbage in the microwave – and the meal is ready to serve in 15 minutes.

Follow the instructions

The first and most important factor is to *read the instruction book* which comes with your microwave. Always keep this on hand for reference – models differ in power and in the way the controls are marked – and follow it as you start to cook. Begin with something simple and straightforward – reheat a cup of coffee, cook a jacket potato or a dish of sliced courgettes – and gradually, you will get used to this new form of cooking method and gain confidence.

If you do have a series of disasters – and there's no reason why you should – don't despair and give up. Try to think logically where you might have gone wrong, refer back to your manufacturer's handbook and the control panel on your cooker and don't be afraid to try again. Remember that the dishes you use will affect the cooking time – some allow food to cook more quickly than others – and that food taken straight from the refrigerator will not cook as quickly as food at room temperature. Foods with a high fat, water or sugar content (bacon, tomatoes, a mincemeat tart) will cook more quickly than denser foods, such as root vegetables.

The amount of energy in a microwave cooker is shared amongst all the food and, unlike in direct heat, the more food there is inside the cooker, the longer it will take. It's a common misconception to think that six potatoes will take the same amount of time as two potatoes: they won't – they'll take longer and they don't have those lovely crisp skins. A useful rule of thumb is to add half the time again for roughly twice the recipe quantity. (Timings for potatoes are on page 99).

The best policy when first starting to 'cook microwave' is to follow the recipe exactly, then once you have mastered it, make notes on the timing, the dishes you have used, and any variation you then make to suit your family's own particular likes and dislikes.

What does a microwave do best?

FISH: I think the microwave really excels at cooking fish; in a remarkably short time, the fish stays tender and moist and the flavour is enhanced. Take care not to overcook it.

MEAT: I have most success in cooking minced beef or lamb, chicken, ham and bacon joints. It is important to remember always to choose good quality cuts of meat for microwave cooking, as the speed and method does not tenderize tougher cuts. Casseroles can take as long to cook – on a **medium** setting – as in the conventional oven.

VEGETABLES: most vegetables give excellent results. Cooked in this way, they retain their fresh flavour, bright colour and don't lose all their goodness in the cooking liquid, since only a small amount of water is needed. They cook mainly in their own juices and taste delicious.

SAUCES: this really has never been so easy! For most sauces, all the ingredients can be measured into a bowl, given a quick whisk, then cooked unattended and whisked again thoroughly before serving. There are no sticky pans to wash as sauces can also be made in the jug from which they are served.

SOUPS: the microwave is splendid for making or reheating small quantities of soup to serve as a first course, or for a light lunch.

DEFROSTING: can be a real life-saver when you have forgotten to take a dish out of the freezer in the morning, ready for supper at night. The microwave will defrost foods quickly and safely.

REHEATING: this is definitely the most efficient and economical way of reheating foods. The dish tastes really freshly cooked, and there is no need to preheat a conventional oven for this.

COOKING FOR ONE OR TWO: the microwave excels at thawing, cooking or reheating small amounts quickly and well. With planning, for one person, this can all be done at the same time, arranged on the same plate for the main course, with just one extra dish for the pudding – less need for a conventional hob and oven (with the consequent fuel-saving) or sticky pans.

My less-than-favourite microwaved foods

ROASTING: as I have indicated, I prefer not to roast beef or pork in the microwave as I find the results are often tougher than I would like, and unattractive in appearance. However, pork crackling gets very crisp if cooked separately in the microwave (see page 65). Lamb does better than either beef or pork, to my taste, but on the whole the family prefer it done in the conventional way.

BREAD AND CAKES: I find it difficult to get used to their generally pasty appearance – that is, unless they are iced or topped and wrapped in clear film straightaway. They really should be eaten on the day of baking as they do tend to stale quickly. Ginger or chocolate-flavoured cakes are much better, though, as they look good and the flavour is fine – my recipes are on page 137.

Larger quantities

More often than not, large quantities take just as long to cook in the microwave as they do 'normally' in the conventional oven. I find it best, therefore, to stick to small quantities which work well and use my microwave for what it does best.

Crisping and browning foods

Dishes with cheese toppings, potato or pastry tops and bread-crumbs sprinkled over can first be cooked in the microwave, then finished off under a hot grill to brown them and make them more palatable in both texture and appearance. (We tend to like our 'crisp' foods to *be* crisp!) A preheated grill makes a good 'finisher' for a microwaved dish.

How long will foods take to cook?

Your instruction booklet that comes with your microwave is your best guide. However, bear the following points in mind, as each will affect the total cooking time:

THE SHAPE AND THICKNESS OF THE DISH: this will alter the cooking time of the food – thick, earthenware dishes will protect the food from the waves and add a few seconds to the cooking time, whereas thinner, microproof thermoplastic dishes will allow the waves to penetrate more easily and reach the food quicker. Square dishes are not so good as microwaves seem to concentrate their energy in the corners (you can shield these with small pieces of foil as long as the foil *does not touch* the sides of the cooker cavity). Where possible choose round or ring-shaped dishes for cooking, as these will give the most even results.

THE TEMPERATURE OF THE FOOD BEFORE COOKING: food taken straight from the refrigerator will naturally take longer to cook than food that is already at room temperature. All frozen foods, with the exception of vegetables, should be defrosted thoroughly *before* cooking. (Some microwave cookers will do this automatically, then go on to calculate the cooking time for you.) It saves energy to think ahead and thaw most things out overnight, in a cupboard in the kitchen (safe from pets) but, of course, you can also thaw a little ahead in your microwave before cooking.

THE AMOUNT OF FOOD: smaller amounts cook more quickly than larger ones. If you are cooking several individual portions at once (chicken legs, Coquilles St Jacques – page 39), they should be of similar weight, size and shape.

COMPOSITION OF FOOD: different types of food heat up at different rates. Dense foods, as I have mentioned, will take longer to heat through than lighter-textured foods, and foods with a great deal of water, fat or sugar in them will heat up or cook through more quickly than foods without. (This is why, again, when reheating a mince pie, the filling gets very hot before the pastry seems warm. Always test with a skewer.) Meat on the bone cooks quicker than meat off the bone. Thin ends cook more quickly than thicker ends.

The timings in the recipes were tested in a 600-watt cooker, and are a guide (see page 21).

Estimating the cooking time

It is always safer to aim to undercook than overcook, so cook the food in short stages, testing each time you take the dish from the cooker. It is always possible to give the food a little longer, but once it has been overcooked there is little that can be done to rescue it. Always cook for the shortest stated time and test with a fork or skewer. Remember to allow for the dish to finish cooking during a short period of standing time.

Estimating the power level for cooking

As a general rule, food which can be cooked at high temperatures (such as foods which normally require boiling) can be cooked at **Full Power** (100%). More delicate foods, such as egg custards, should be cooked on **Medium** (50%) or **Low/Defrost** (30%), as they would be on a lower setting in the conventional cooker. In a microwave, though, it is misleading to think of temperature (heat). Though foods get hot, they are cooked by bursts of microwave energy.

Foods unsuitable for microwaving

To my mind, meringues are far better if made in the conventional way. Don't attempt to hard-boil eggs (they can be done, if the shells are pricked, they are wrapped in foil and immersed in water, but it's such a fiddle . . .), make Yorkshire Puddings (they won't rise), or deep-fry anything in hot fat (you can't control the temperature).

Cooking techniques

IF YOUR MICROWAVE HAS A TURNTABLE, rearrange foods halfway through cooking by turning them sides-to-middle. Place a single dish in the centre of the turntable, or arrange individual dishes or portions evenly spaced in a circle round the edge of the turntable. Microwaves cook the outsides first and tend to fizzle out as they reach the centre of the cooker. This is why you should always arrange foods with the thickest part to the outside, and the thinner ends towards the centre.

IF YOUR MICROWAVE HAS NO TURNTABLE, reposition the food two or three times during cooking, in addition to following the guidelines above. This helps the food to cook evenly and guards against the 'hot spots' which some cookers do have.

STIRRING AND TURNING AND REARRANGING: always stir foods regularly during cooking. Turn the dish, or the pieces of food, to the centre halfway through the cooking time and hold the lid and shake the dish to level out something like a cauliflower as it is cooking. Whisk sauces, too, after cooking.

SHIELDING: always shield thin end, heads and tails of fish etc. with small strips of foil. Microwaves cannot pass through metal and the food is therefore kept from further cooking.

EVEN SHAPES: foods of an even thickness cook better, so arrange wedge-shaped portions alternately, tuck ends of fillets underneath the thicker part of a fish, or protect the thinner ends as above.

COVERING: cover any foods which usually require a moist cooking method (vegetables, casseroles) with a layer of clear film or a lid. Always make sure there is room for steam, which collects under the lid, to escape during cooking (some micro- wave cookers calculate the cooking time automatically by 'sensing' the amount of steam in the cooking cavity). Turn back a corner of the film, or pierce it in several places with a fork or knife. Make sure that a lid is not tight-fitting.

To prevent foods from bursting

As steam collects inside foods just under the skin, always prick those foods which have a membrane or skin (egg yolks, sausages, whole potatoes) with a fork or cocktail stick, other- wise they will burst. Always slash the skins of whole fish, too, in two or three places or they will also burst under the pressure of the steam inside.

Cooking equipment

As a general rule, cookware which is dishwasher-proof is suitable for the microwave. Test cookware for the first time by placing a glass jug half-filled with water in the microwave. Put the dish beside it and cook on **full power** setting for about 30 seconds. If, at the end of this time, the water is warm and the dish is hot, the dish isn't suitable for use. If, however, the dish is still cool, then it should be fine *provided* it has no metallic (gold or silver) decoration on it.

ANY HEAT-RESISTANT GLASS COOKWARE: this is ideal for micro- wave cooking, and it is likely that most of us already have a good selection in the kitchen. Pyrex and Visionware are probably the most common and include measuring jugs, mixing bowls, cov- ered casseroles, pie plates. Perhaps the only disadvantage of using mixing bowls and jugs is that the food may need to be transferred to a warm serving dish to take to the table.

CHINA AND POTTERY: many different makes of china and dinnerware are safe to use in the microwave, but to be on the safe side, check with the manufacturer's care leaflet first. **Do not use** anything with a metallic trimming, i.e. with gold rims, or those marked 'ironstone' as these have metal in the glaze and are not microwave-safe.

PLASTICS: plastic containers are useful for short reheating or defrosting periods. However, they must be thick, or the heat from food will cause them to turn soft and distort. Best to use containers specially made for microwave cooking obtainable by mail order from Lakeland Plastics, Alexandra Buildings, Windermere, Cumbria LA23 1BQ. Tel: (09662) 2257.

SPOONS AND UTENSILS: wooden spoons and sturdy plastic utensils can be used for stirring and left in the microwave for a *short* while. Use wooden skewers for kebabs and wooden cocktail sticks for securing stuffings inside. Never, ever put metal utensils in the cooker, or they will cause 'arcing' and could damage the magnetron.

Specially designed microwave containers

There is now a huge range of containers available for use in the microwave, the quality of which varies considerably as do the prices. Before purchasing any items you think you need, get to know your microwave and find out where the gaps are in the equipment you already have. It makes no sense to buy a whole range of different-shaped dishes when you can use some of the equipment you already possess.

WAVEWARE COOKING SET: my favourite, most used piece of microwave equipment is a three-piece cooking set which includes a high round dome, a roasting rack and a lid. This huge dome can either be used as a bowl for jams, casseroles, soups and rice dishes, or as a cover when roasting meats. Being so large, the food being cooked doesn't boil over. The lid is also dual-purpose since it can be used to cover the dome when cooking moist dishes, or it can act as a container on its own for hamburgers, fish and other 'dry' foods. The rack fits neatly inside the lid and lifts joints of meat or poultry above their juices to prevent them boiling during cooking. I also invested in a browning skillet and a loaf-shaped container.

BROWNING SKILLET: this allows small pieces of food which are normally grilled or shallow-fried to be cooked and browned in the microwave. It needs to be preheated for about 6 minutes before cooking and the food will then brown from the heat of the dish (it has a special coating) and also be cooked by microwave: for sausages, bacon and toasted sandwiches.

LOAF-SHAPED DISHES: useful for meat loaves, pâtés, loaves and teabreads. Ideally, choose one with well-rounded corners as this helps to ensure more even cooking, unless you shield them with small pieces of foil.

FOR BAKING: I suggest you buy a ring-shaped container, and one or two items to suit your particular needs. Conventional tins cannot be used in the microwave. As with all new kitchen equipment, do read and follow the manufacturer's instructions with care.

WRAPS AND BAGS: moist foods must be covered during cooking, otherwise they turn dry and unacceptable. Coverings, whether a lid or clear film, help to prevent any loss of moisture by evaporation.

CLEAR FILM: ideal for covering containers which do not have their own lids, can also be used for lining containers. Pierce, if used as a covering, or turn back one corner, leaving enough room to stir through the aperture. Do take great care when lifting film off a cooked dish as it will release an extremely hot steam cloud which could scald.

ALUMINIUM FOIL: only use in small quantities for shielding food to prevent overcooking.

ROASTING BAGS: excellent for roasting joints of meat and poultry, also for par-cooking potatoes in the microwave before roasting them in a conventional oven. Do not use wire ties to secure the ends; nylon ties are ideal, otherwise use an elastic band or piece of string.

POLYTHENE BAGS: useful for cooking vegetables or blanching them for the freezer.

COOK-IN BAGS: many frozen, prepacked convenience foods come in these. They are safe to use in the microwave so long as they are pierced in the top to prevent them from bursting open during cooking.

KITCHEN PAPER: use for covering fatty foods such as bacon, which are likely to spit during cooking, but which should not be covered with clear film. Use for reheating pastry items, such as sausage rolls. The paper absorbs any fat and prevents them becoming soggy. (Also useful for drying herbs and drying petals for pot pourri.)

PAPER NAPKINS: for warming bread rolls or reheating foods such as hamburgers or hot dogs which are to be eaten in the fingers.

Defrosting foods in the microwave

Any type of food can be successfully defrosted in the microwave whether meat, fish, prepared dishes, soups, or vegetables. Defrosting times may vary slightly depending on the power level of your particular microwave so do keep an eye on foods whilst they are defrosting and alter the timing accordingly.

Remove food from foil or metal containers and transfer it to a microwave-safe container; also remember to remove any metal ties.

If, during defrosting, a particular area of the food begins to feel warm, shield this with a small piece of foil whilst the rest of the food is defrosting.

With delicate foods such as frozen fruit or fish, I find it best to partially thaw the food and then to let it finish thawing during the standing period. Fruit then doesn't start to lose its shape and fish doesn't begin to cook.

Vegetables do not need defrosting before they are cooked and can be heated on **full power** straight from frozen. All vegetables should be covered, and stirred during cooking; it is not necessary to add additional water when cooking vegetables straight from frozen.

When defrosting large items such as a piece of meat or small turkey, it is best to defrost it in two or three stages and allow a standing time in between. If this is not done the outside may begin to cook and the middle remain frozen.

Baked products such as bread and cakes take very little time to defrost – perfect when you have forgotten to take a loaf out of the freezer at breakfast time!

Reheating foods in the microwave

On the whole, **full power** is used and food is quickly heated through with very little effort. Do remember to allow it to stand for a few moments before serving, so that the residual heat spreads evenly throughout the food.

'PLATE MEALS': arrange the food on the plate with the thickest parts to the outside and thinner, more delicate parts towards the middle. As far as possible, the food should be of even shapes and sizes; if you are serving a large potato, cut this into smaller pieces to balance with the other foods. Cover to cook.

COOKED DISHES: fish pies or lasagnes may be cooked well ahead and then reheat as required. Do remember to allow slightly longer heating time if the dish has been taken straight from the refrigerator. Cover to cook.

SOUPS: heat in compact containers which will allow for stirring; these heat much more quickly than a broad, shallow container. Cook covered and stir during reheating.

VEGETABLES: can be cooked ahead, arranged attractively on serving dishes and then covered and reheated to serve. It may be necessary to stir or rearrange the vegetables during reheating to ensure they heat through evenly.

CASSEROLES AND STEWS: cover to cook and stir once or twice from the sides to the middle during reheating.

Safety first

Remember to leave a cup of water in the microwave when it is not in use, then if it is switched on accidentally, the magnetron which produces the microwaves will not be damaged. And *always* be wary of scalding yourself in the hot steam that can gush out from under a layer of clear film (even if it has been pierced) or a lid. Be sure (and tell the children) always to remove the covering from the side of the dish farthest from you *first*.

IMPORTANT
The recipes in this book were tested in a Panasonic Genius 600-watt-output cooker with a turntable. If your particular model has a 400–500-watt output (i.e. slightly less power), allow an extra 20 seconds per minute; if your microwave is a 700-watt output model, subtract 15 seconds per minute from the recipe timings. You will soon be able to calculate timings to your taste. (REMINDER: cookers do vary and the size and shape of the dish will affect the cooking time.)

Breakfast!

I must admit it's a boon to be able to take the butter straight from the fridge first thing in the morning and heat it on the **defrost** setting of my microwave for 20–30 seconds. It's then just right for spreading on toast or rolls without tearing up the bread. This is just one of the many ways my microwave now helps me start the day on the right foot! I heat up the milk for the cereal – and it doesn't stick to the pan, and there's no longer an excuse for wasting cold coffee or leftover toast. It can be quickly reheated for elevenses.

It only takes a few seconds to heat up bread rolls, too, but I find the bread stales very quickly once it has been warmed or thawed out in the microwave. So I'm now very careful to take out just enough for the family breakfast . . . I learnt the hard way, though, when I tried to defrost a whole loaf at breakfast time, only to find it dried out and couldn't be used for sandwiches later in the day – just toast, and lots and lots of breadcrumbs.

And as the family grows up and eats in relays, the micro-wave is very handy for making single portions.

Here are our favourite traditional breakfasts.

PORRIDGE

Power Level: Full   **Cooking Time:** 5 Minutes
Serves 1

2oz (50g) quick porridge oats   sugar or honey and milk, to
¼ pint (150ml) milk   serve
¼ pint (150ml) water

*It may not be faster to make porridge in the microwave, but it is
far easier and there are no sticky pans to clean up!*

Measure the oats, milk and water into a deep microproof
serving bowl. Mix well and cook on **full power** for 5 minutes,
stirring twice during cooking and again at the end of the
cooking time. Serve straightaway with sugar or honey and
milk, to taste.

KIPPERS

Power Level: Full   **Cooking Time:** 4 Minutes
Serves 2

2 kipper fillets
a generous knob of butter

*Serve for breakfast or light lunch. Do take care not to overcook
the fish since kippers cook in such a short time.*

Arrange the kippers in a microproof dish, add the butter, cover with a lid or pierced clear film and cook on **full power** for 4 minutes, or until the flesh flakes easily.

SCRAMBLED EGGS AND BACON

Power Level: Full   **Cooking Time:** 6 Minutes
Serves 2

4 rashers lean, rindless bacon   salt
4 eggs   freshly ground black pepper
2 tablespoons milk   1oz (25g) butter

Bacon cooks extremely well in the microwave like this, without any mess, and it retains its flavour.

With scissors, finely snip the bacon into a bowl and cook on **full power** for 2 minutes. Beat the eggs with the milk, seasoning and butter. Pour over the bacon and cook on **full power** for 2 minutes. Stir thoroughly. Cook on **full power** for a further minute, then stir. Cook for a final minute and stir again before serving with hot buttered toast.

WHOLE ENGLISH BREAKFAST

Power Level: Full   **Cooking Time:** 10 Minutes
Serves 2

2 sausages, skins pricked   2 eggs
2 rashers rindless bacon   2 tomatoes

Everything is cooked together in a browning dish or skillet, so there's much less washing up! Prick the sausages and egg yolks, or they burst.

Preheat the empty browning dish or skillet for 6 minutes on **full power**. Arrange the sausages on the hot skillet and cook for 2 minutes, then turn them over. Add bacon rashers and eggs. Prick the egg yolks with a cocktail stick. Cook on **full power** for a further minute. Turn over the bacon and push to one side. Add tomatoes and cook for 1 more minute then serve straightaway.

CRUNCHY MUESLI

Power Level: Full   **Cooking Time:** 3–5 Minutes
Serves 4

6oz (175g) rolled oats
2oz (50g) hazelnuts or almonds
2 tablespoons sesame seeds
2 tablespoons wheatgerm

4 tablespoons runny honey
2 tablespoons sunflower oil
2oz (50g) raisins
2oz (50g) dried apricots, chopped

For the health-conscious (especially the children these days) you can make your own muesli quickly and crisp it up in the microwave. Serve the basic mixture, varying the quantities to suit your taste, with chopped fresh fruits in season.

Measure the oats into a bowl with the nuts, sesame seeds and wheatgerm. Stir in the honey and sunflower oil and mix well. Spread the mixture evenly in a shallow microproof dish or plate and cook on **full power** for 3 to 5 minutes, stirring every minute until the muesli browns evenly and the oats are nicely toasted.

Add the raisins and apricots, allow to cool and serve with milk and chopped fresh fruits.

Note: for a drier muesli mix, stir the oats, nuts and sesame seeds together in a shallow bowl with light muscovado sugar to taste, then stir and cook on **full power** until the oats and nuts are toasted. Stir in the rest of the ingredients you fancy and serve with milk and fresh fruit. This basic mixture should store well in an airtight tin.

Crispening breakfast cereals

Breakfast cereals popped into a bowl lined with kitchen paper can be revived after only 30 seconds on **full power**. Depending on staleness, it may take up to 3 minutes, cooking in 30 second bursts. Stand a cup of water in the microwave to prevent the kitchen paper from overheating.

Soups and Starters

As a family, we are fond of soups: they make great standbys for lunch when the weather turns chilly – and starters are very useful, too, when entertaining. They make a good first course for a Sunday lunch, or turn into lunch or supper dishes for less formal occasions.

The microwave can help in lots of ways to speed up preparation as well as cooking: lentils and dried pulses no longer need pre-soaking, gelatine can be dissolved quickly and easily for mousses, and dishes can be made ahead of time and thawed or reheated at the very last moment. It certainly helps when planning a meal to know that each course can be served piping hot and at the right time (without having to leave the dish in the oven to keep warm, often when you are cooking something else on a higher temperature).

Most of the soups and starters I have included can be prepared a few hours ahead of time – some even the day before – and simply reheated for serving. I have found it is best to heat up soups in a tall, deep, narrow container rather than a wide, shallow one – as long as you have room for stirring during reheating, and at the end of the cooking time before being served.

And a latecomer need not cause problems. Simply set out an individual portion and leave it ready for quick reheating when they arrive.

MAKING GOOD STOCK

I still firmly believe that the basis of a good soup is a well-flavoured stock. Now a stockpot usually needs long, slow cooking and stock-making is often best left to the conventional cooker. However, if you are short of time, I have found it *is* possible to make stock in the microwave, especially if you make a concentrated one. Place the meat bones, any vegetables (carrot, onion, celery), a little seasoning, herbs and water in a large microproof bowl. Cover with a lid or pierced clear film and cook on **medium power** for 30 minutes, or on **low power** (or the **defrost** setting) for up to 2 hours. Strain, discard the bones and vegetables and use the stock as required. It should be good and flavoursome.

SIMPLE TOMATO SOUP

Power Level: Full   **Cooking Time:** 12 Minutes
Serves 2–3

1oz (25g) butter
2 small onions, finely
  chopped
1oz (25g) flour
½ pint (300ml) water
2½oz (62g) can tomato purée
½ pint (300ml) milk

1 teaspoon caster sugar
salt
freshly ground black pepper
a little chopped parsley
  (optional)
grated Parmesan cheese for
  sprinkling

Quick and easy to make – with ingredients from the storecupboard.

Melt the butter in a microproof bowl on **full power** for 1 minute, add the onion, mix well and cook for 3 minutes. Stir in the flour, then gradually blend in the water, tomato purée, milk, sugar and seasoning. Cover with a lid or pierced clear film and cook on **full power** for 8 minutes, stirring twice during cooking. Remove from cooker. Stir again and taste to check seasoning. Pour into serving bowls and serve sprinkled with Parmesan cheese and parsley.

VEGETABLE SOUP

Power Level: Full   **Cooking Time:** 32 minutes
Serves 6

1oz (25g) butter
1lb (450g) onions, sliced
1 large potato, peeled and
    evenly diced
4oz (100g) carrots, sliced
4oz (100g) cauliflower, cut
    into small florets

4oz (100g) spinach, torn into
    small pieces
1½ pints (900ml) good stock
salt
freshly ground black pepper

A quick and healthy meal; if liked, make it in advance, set aside, then thin down with a little extra stock when reheating.

Put the butter in a large microproof bowl and heat on **full power** for 1 minute. Add the onions and cook on **full power** for a further 3 minutes. Add the remaining vegetables, stock and seasoning. Cover with a lid or pierced clear film and cook on **full power** for 20 minutes, or until the vegetables are tender. Blend in a processor or blender until smooth. Taste to check the seasoning.

Return the soup to the bowl, thin down with a little extra stock, if liked. Reheat until piping hot to serve. This will take about 8 minutes on **full power** if reheating from cold, less if the soup is still a little warm.

CREAMY MUSHROOM SOUP

Power Level: Full   **Cooking Time:** 21 Minutes
Serves 4

1 small onion, chopped
1 tablespoon sunflower oil
8oz (225g) mushrooms or
    mushroom stalks, chopped
2oz (50g) flour

1¼ pints (750ml) chicken
    stock
salt
freshly ground black pepper
¼ pint (300ml) milk

If possible, buy mushroom stalks for this recipe; they can sometimes be found very reasonably in greengrocers.

Put the onion into a microproof bowl, measure in the oil and mix well. Cover with a lid or pierced clear film and cook on **full power** for 5 minutes; add the mushrooms, stir, cover again and cook for a further 3 minutes.

Stir in the flour until thoroughly blended, then gradually blend in the stock, stirring well. Stir in the seasoning and cook on **full power** for 8 minutes, stirring once during cooking.

Reduce the soup to a purée in a processor or blender, then return it to the bowl with the milk. Heat on **full power** for about 5 minutes until piping hot.

Taste to check the seasoning, and stir in a little extra milk if the soup seems a little too thick.

Turn into a warmed tureen to serve.

BACON AND SPINACH SOUP

Power Levels: Full and Medium
Cooking Time: 30 Minutes   **Serves 6**

1 large onion, chopped
2 tablespoons sunflower oil
6oz (175g) streaky bacon, de-rinded and chopped
1lb (450g) frozen spinach, thawed
1oz (25g) flour

¾ pint (450ml) milk
¾ pint (450ml) chicken stock
1 tablespoon Worcestershire sauce
salt
freshly ground black pepper
¼ pint (150ml) single cream

Very good to serve when the weather is really chilly outside! You can thaw the spinach in the microwave.

Put the onion into a microproof bowl, measure in the oil and add the bacon. Mix well. Cover with a lid or pierced clear film and cook on **full power** for 5 minutes. Add the spinach, cover again, and cook on **medium power** for 5 minutes.

Stir the flour into the spinach and mix well, then gradually blend into the milk and stock. Add the Worcestershire sauce and seasoning, cover and cook on **full power** for 5 minutes. Stir well, then return to the cooker on **medium power** for a further 10 minutes.

Purée the soup in a processor or blender. Return to the bowl, and heat, uncovered, on **full power** for 5 minutes, or until piping hot. Taste to check the seasoning, then stir in all but 1 tablespoon of the cream.

Turn into a tureen and swirl the remaining cream over the top. Serve at once.

MILD CURRIED PARSNIP SOUP

Power Levels: Full and Medium
Cooking Time: 18 Minutes　　**Serves** 6

1 onion, chopped
1lb (450g) parsnips, cubed
2 tablespoons sunflower oil
1 good tablespoon flour
1 good teaspoon curry powder
2 pints (1.2 litres) good stock,
  heated to boiling point

salt
freshly ground black pepper

To serve
¼ pint (150ml) single cream
freshly snipped chives

For an instant fruit soup, add 2lb (900g) peeled, cored and sliced Bramley apples to the soup instead of the parsnips. This makes a delicious variation.

Put the onion and parsnip into a large microproof bowl. Measure in the oil and stir so the vegetables are evenly coated. Cover with a lid or pierced clear film and cook on **full power** for 5 minutes.

Stir in the flour and curry powder, then gradually blend in the boiling stock. Add seasoning, cover and cook on **medium power** for 10 minutes, or until the parsnips are tender, stirring once during cooking.

Reduce the soup to a purée in a processor or blender – it may be necessary to do this in batches. Return the soup to the bowl, cover and reheat on **full power** for about 3 minutes, or until piping hot.

Stir in the cream, taste to check the seasoning, then serve sprinkled with freshly snipped chives.

Note: it's quicker to boil the stock on top of the stove in the conventional way before adding it to the soup.

RED LENTIL SOUP

Power Level: Full   **Cooking Time:** 23 Minutes
Serves 4

1 onion, chopped	1½ pints (900ml) good stock
1 carrot, diced	1 bay leaf
2 sticks celery, trimmed and sliced	salt
2 tablespoons sunflower oil	1 level teaspoon paprika pepper
4oz (100g) red lentils	a good pinch Cayenne pepper

Here's a good way of spinning out those few odd vegetables you might happen to find in the bottom of the fridge into a warming and satisfying soup. There's no need to pre-soak the lentils.

Put the onion, carrot and celery into a microproof bowl with the oil. Mix well, then cook on **full power** for 5 minutes, until the vegetables are beginning to soften. Add lentils and 1 pint (600ml) of the stock, the bay leaf and seasonings. Cover with a lid or pierced clear film and cook on **full power** for 15 minutes, or until lentils and vegetables are tender. Remove and discard the bay leaf.

Pour soup into a processor or blender and reduce to a purée – it may be necessary to do this in two batches. Return to the bowl, stir in the remaining ½ pint (300ml) stock and taste to check the seasoning.

Reheat on **full power** for about 3 minutes until piping hot to serve.

HOT GRAPEFRUIT

Power Level: Medium   **Cooking Time:** 3 Minutes
Serves 4

2 grapefruit
1 small jar preserved ginger
  in syrup

4 teaspoons light muscovado
  sugar

There are many variations of this recipe; try topping with mint jelly or runny honey and nuts before heating.

Cut the grapefruit in half and cut around inside each half to loosen the flesh. Cut down between the segments and remove any pith and white skin. Pour a tablespoon of ginger syrup over each grapefruit half and sprinkle each with a teaspoon of sugar.

Cut the pieces of ginger in thin slices and arrange them around the edge of the grapefruit; fill the centre with chopped ginger. Arrange evenly spaced in a microproof dish and heat on **medium power** for 3 minutes, or until the grapefruit has heated through. Serve straightaway.

MUSHROOMS À LA CRÈME

Power Level: Full   **Cooking Time:** 8 Minutes
Serves 4

12oz (350g) small button
  mushrooms
1½oz (40g) butter
1 fat clove garlic, crushed

salt
freshly ground black pepper
¼ pint (150ml) double cream

Use small white fresh button mushrooms for this dish. Cook and serve straightaway.

Wipe the mushrooms and trim the ends off the stalks. Heat the butter in a microproof bowl on **full power** for 1 minute, add garlic and mushrooms, then stir and cook on **full power** for 4 minutes. Season well, stir in the cream and cook on **full power** for 3 minutes. Divide between 4 small dishes and serve.

COQUILLES ST JACQUES

Power Level: Full   **Cooking Time:** 15 Minutes
Serves 6

6 scallops	salt
½ pint (300ml) dry cider	freshly ground black pepper
	12oz (350g) creamy mashed
For the sauce	potato
1oz (25g) butter	a few browned breadcrumbs
1oz (25g) flour	parsley to garnish

You can prepare these ahead of time and keep them in the refrigerator. Reheat them to serve.

Remove the scallops from their shells, wash thoroughly and remove the beards. Place in a microproof bowl with the cider, cover with a lid or pierced clear film and cook on **full power** for 6 minutes. Lift out the scallops with a slotted spoon and reserve the cooking liquor for the sauce. Slice the scallops.

To make the sauce, heat the butter in a bowl on **full power** for 1 minute, stir in the flour, then gradually blend in the scallop cooking liquor. Heat on **full power** for 3 minutes, stirring twice during cooking and whisking well at the end of cooking until the sauce is smooth and thickened. Add sliced scallops and seasoning to taste.

Form a border of potato around each of the scallop shells. Fill the centres with a spoonful of the sauce and sprinkle the breadcrumbs over.

To serve, heat on **full power** for 5 minutes, then transfer to a hot grill until top of potato is pale golden brown. Sprinkle with parsley and serve at once.

SALMON MOUSSES

Power Level: Full **Cooking Time:** 5 Minutes
Serves 8

12oz (350g) fresh salmon
1oz (25g) gelatine
4 tablespoons cold water
10½oz (298g) can condensed consommé soup
½ pint (300ml) double cream, whipped
¾ pint (450ml) good thick mayonnaise

juice of 1 lemon
salt
freshly ground black pepper
1 tablespoon freshly chopped parsley
chopped fresh dill to garnish (optional)

These look pretty served in individual dishes garnished with fresh dill. Serve with granary bread and salad.

Arrange the salmon in a cooking dish, cover and cook on **full power** for 4 minutes. Flake the fish.

Put the gelatine in a microproof bowl with the water and leave for 5 minutes to form a sponge, then heat on **full power** for 1 minute to dissolve the gelatine. Allow to cool slightly, then stir in the consommé. In another bowl, blend the cream, mayonnaise and lemon juice together, then fold in the cooked flaked salmon and three-quarters of the consommé. Taste to check the seasoning. Divide the mixture between eight ramekin dishes and leave to set.

Stir the parsley into the remaining consommé, heating a little in the microwave if necessary, and carefully spoon over the mousse. Chill until required and serve decorated with dill.

Favourite Fish
(and Shellfish)

Fish has a delicate, tender flesh and needs only the minimum of cooking. It is a perfect food for microwaving and I now find I prefer to cook my fish in the microwave for everything – except frying. It doesn't seem to matter whether I'm cooking the fish very simply – with lemon or lime juice and herbs from the garden – or combining it with a sauce to produce a fish pie; the results are always excellent. It is essential, though, to check the fish a minute or so *before* you think it should be ready as it can quickly overcook and the flesh loses texture. Cook it just until the outside is opaque and the middle is still a little translucent (test by flaking a little with a fork). It will finish cooking on standing – leaving just long enough to decorate the dish, or finish off the vegetables to serve with it.

It is important, when microwaving, to arrange the fish correctly, or it cooks unevenly (see next page). Whole fillets will cook more quickly at the thinner end, so this must be shielded, or folded under to make a neat and even shape.

I find it so much easier to skin a fish after microwaving; the skin seems to fall away from the flesh without tearing it. This is such an advantage if you have planned to serve, say, cold trout with a salad for a summer party. Cook the fish ahead, skin and decorate it and leave it in a cool place until you are ready to serve it. For larger fish, such as a whole salmon, cut off the head and the tail fillet so it will fit into the cooker, cook the ends separately, then decorate the joins with cucumber slices and no-one will be any wiser.

Always season fish with salt after cooking, otherwise it toughens the flesh.

BASIC METHODS OF COOKING FISH

To 'steam' fish

Arrange the fish in the dish with the thickest parts to the outside. Moisten a piece of kitchen paper with water and place loosely over the top of the fish. Cook just until the flesh flakes easily. Allow to stand.

To cook fish steaks

Arrange the fish steaks in the dish with the meaty parts towards the outside edge. Tuck any flaps under to form a neat and even shape. Add lemon juice or a little butter, cover and cook just until the flesh flakes easily. Allow to stand.

To cook whole fish

For small fish, arrange in a dish with the tails overlapping in the centre of the dish; for larger fish, lay them side by side, facing in opposite directions. Shield the head and tail with little pieces of foil. Slash the skin 2–3 times with a sharp knife to prevent the skin from bursting during cooking, then cover and cook for the recommended time.

To cook fish fillets in a sauce

Arrange the fillets in the dish with the thickest parts to the outside, pour the sauce over, then cover and cook just until the flesh flakes easily.

Recommended cooking times

FISH FILLETS: allow 5–7 minutes per lb (450g) on **full power**.
FISH STEAKS: allow 4–5 minutes per lb (450g) on **full power**.
WHOLE FISH: allow 6–8 minutes per lb (450g) on **full power**.

BEURRE MANIÉ (KNEADED BUTTER)

Blend together 8oz (225g) softened butter and 8oz (225g) flour. Store in the refrigerator until required. Whisk the specified amount into hot liquids at the end of the cooking time to thicken. Beurre manié (kneaded butter) is perfect for finishing soups, sauces and casseroles. (You can soften the butter on **medium power** in the microwave.)

BAKED CUTLETS WITH CHEESE AND TOMATO TOPPING

Power Level: Full   **Cooking Time:** 10–12 Minutes
Serves 4

4 cod cutlets
4 tomatoes, skinned and
  sliced
½ pint (300ml) milk
2oz (50g) beurre manié (see
  above)

salt
freshly ground black pepper
4oz (100g) well-flavoured
  Cheddar cheese, grated

Serve with fresh green broccoli for a light, healthy lunch or supper dish.

Arrange the cutlets in a microproof dish with the tomato slices on top. Heat the milk in an ovenproof glass jug on **full power** for about 2 minutes, then whisk in the beurre manié until the sauce is smooth and thickened. Season to taste with salt and pepper and pour over the fish. Top with the grated cheese.

Cook on **full power** for 8–10 minutes, then transfer to a hot grill for a minute or two until the cheese is golden brown and bubbling.

PLAICE FLORENTINE

Power Level: Full   **Cooking Time:** 12 Minutes
Serves 4, or 8 as a first course

8 small fillets of plaice,
    skinned
salt
freshly ground black pepper
juice of ½ lemon
1 pint (600ml) milk
4oz (100g) beurre manié
    (page 44)

1lb (450g) frozen cut-leaf
    spinach, cooked as directed
    on the packet
2oz (50g) well-flavoured
    Cheddar cheese, grated
1oz (25g) fresh white
    breadcrumbs

There is no need to cook the fish before the dish is assembled. It will cook to perfection without this.

Season the fish fillets with a little salt and pepper and sprinkle with lemon juice; roll them up. Heat the milk in a microproof jug on **full power** for about 4 minutes, then whisk in the beurre manié until smooth and thickened. Season to taste. Blend about 6 tablespoons of the sauce with the spinach and spoon into a microproof serving dish.

Arrange the fish rolls on top of the bed of spinach and spoon over the remaining sauce. Mix the cheese and breadcrumbs together and sprinkle over the sauce.

To serve, heat on **full power** for 8 minutes, then transfer to a hot grill until the topping is golden brown.

Extracting juice from citrus fruits
Grate rind first, if using. Cut fruit in half, place cut side down on an ovenglass plate. Microwave 2 minutes on **full power** and the juice flows out – with no squeezing.

FAMILY FISH PIE

Power Level: Full   **Cooking Time:** 18 Minutes
Serves 4–6

1lb (450g) cod fillets
1 pint (600ml) milk
4oz (100g) beurre manié
  (page 44)
salt
freshly ground black pepper

2 tablespoons chopped fresh
  parsley
a little nutmeg
4 hard-boiled eggs, quartered
1½lb (675g) creamy mashed
  potato

A great standby for a Saturday family lunch; make it the day before and heat through when required.

Arrange the fish fillets in a dish, cover with a lid or pierced clear film and cook on **full power** for 6 minutes until the flesh flakes easily. Peel off and discard skin and remove any bones.

Heat the milk in a bowl on **full power** for about 4 minutes, then whisk in the beurre manié until smooth and thickened. Season the sauce to taste and add parsley, nutmeg to taste, eggs and flaked fish. Turn into a serving dish. Spread the potato carefully over the sauce and mark the top with a fork.

To serve, heat through on **full power** for about 8 minutes, then transfer to a hot grill for a minute or two until the potato has browned. (You can cook a vegetable or two for accompaniment while the potato topping is browning.)

SOLE BONNE FEMME

Power Level: Full   **Cooking Time:** About 12 Minutes
Serves 4

4 shallots or 1 medium onion,
  very finely chopped
4oz (100g) button
  mushrooms, sliced
2oz (50g) butter
4 lemon sole fillets, each
  about 8oz (225g) in weight
4 tablespoons white wine
¼ pt (150ml) fish or chicken
  stock

1–2 tablespoons lemon juice
2 tablespoons chopped fresh
  parsley
1oz (25g) beurre manié
  (page 44)
salt
freshly ground black pepper
lemon slices and chopped
  parsley to garnish

Easy, tasty classic dish – and so quick to prepare. Plaice works well in this recipe, too.

Put the shallots or onion into a microproof bowl with the mushrooms and butter. Cover with pierced clear film and cook on **full power** for 3 minutes. Stir, then spread in an even layer in the bottom of a shallow microproof dish. Roll up the fillets, head to tail, and arrange evenly over the mushroom mixture. Set aside.

Put wine, stock and lemon juice into a jug with the parsley and heat on **full power** until almost boiling – about 3 minutes. Pour over fish, cover with pierced clear film and cook on **full power** for 5 minutes.

Transfer fish to a heated serving dish and spoon round the mushroom mixture with a slotted spoon, reserving a few cooked mushroom slices for garnish. Strain the cooking juices into a jug, whisk in the beurre manié until smooth and thickened, then season well. Reheat for 1 to 2 minutes until bubbling, whisk well and pour over fish.

Decorate with cooked mushroom slices, chopped parsley and lemon twists. Serve with green beans and baby carrots.

TROUT WITH ALMONDS

Power Level: Full   **Cooking Time:** 11 Minutes
Serves 4

4 medium trout, cleaned
1 lemon
2oz (50g) butter

2oz (50g) toasted flaked almonds

Fish retains its full flavour when cooked in the microwave, and this classic favourite is particularly good.

Arrange the trout on a microproof serving dish, two fish facing one way and two facing in the opposite direction. Shield the heads and tails of the fish with small strips of foil, cut 2–3 slits across each fish, cover dish with pierced clear film and cook on **full power** for 8 minutes.

Cut the lemon in half and stand the two halves in the microproof bowl, cut sides facing down. Heat on **full power** for 30 seconds. Squeeze out juice and discard shells. Add butter and almonds to the lemon juice and heat on **full power** for 30 seconds. Mix well and pour over the trout.

Return the fish to the microwave and cook on **full power** for 2 minutes. Serve.

Poached Salmon for a Summer Buffet

Most microwaves will take a salmon, or salmon trout, up to about 3½lb (1.5kg). If the fish is too long, either curl it gently, nose to tail, into a shallow round microproof dish, or cut the head off, cook it at the same time, then mask the join with parsley or cucumber when you serve it.

Cover the thin tail end with a strip of foil and allow a maximum of 4 minutes per lb (450g), testing frequently. Cover the dish with pierced clear film and the fish will cook in its own juices.

When it has cooled a little, take off the skin and arrange the fish on the serving dish. Leave, covered, until you are ready to decorate and serve it – with mayonnaise or Hollandaise Sauce (page 116) and a selection of salads.

KEDGEREE

Power Level: Full   **Cooking Time:** 28 Minutes
Serves 3–4

1 tablespoon sunflower oil
1 large onion, chopped
8oz (225g) long-grain rice
1 pint (600ml) hot chicken stock
1lb (450g) smoked haddock, cooked, skinned and flaked

3 tablespoons freshly chopped parsley
juice of 1 lemon
4 hard-boiled eggs, quartered
salt
freshly ground black pepper

A traditional family favourite, which I often serve for breakfast or lunch at the weekend. Cook the haddock in the microwave in advance.

Measure the oil into a microproof bowl, add the onion and cook on **full power** for 3 minutes. Stir in the rice and stock, cover and cook on **full power** for up to 20 minutes, stirring once during cooking. Add the flaked fish, parsley and lemon juice to the rice and cook, covered, for a further 5 minutes.

Stir in quartered eggs and seasoning to taste, stand for about 3 minutes, then serve.

Note: to remove any lingering cooking smells from the cooker, wipe inside the cavity, put a slice or two of lemon in a cup of cold water and bring to the boil on **full power**. Remove from the cooker and the cooking smells should have gone.

MOULES MARINIÈRE

Power Level: Full   **Cooking Time:** 15 Minutes
Serves 3

2lb (900g) mussels
1oz (25g) butter
1 large onion, chopped
4 stalks parsley
2 sprigs fresh thyme
1 bay leaf
freshly ground black pepper

½ pint (300ml) dry white wine or cider
1oz (25g) beurre manié (page 44)
chopped fresh parsley, to serve

Discard any mussels with shells which are badly chipped or cracked, or any that do not close tightly. Those which remain open are dead and should not be cooked.

Scrape and clean each mussel with a strong knife, removing every trace of seaweed, mud and beard. Wash in several changes of water. Drain well in a colander.

Measure the butter into a large microproof bowl and heat on **full power** for 1 minute, add the onion and cook on **full power** for 3 minutes. Stir in the parsley, thyme, bay leaf, pepper and white wine or cider and cook on **full power** for 5 minutes. Add the mussels to the hot wine, cover and cook on **full power** for

5 minutes. Remove any mussels which have not opened and discard these, together with the empty halves of the shells and the herbs.

Strain off most of the cooking liquid into a jug, heat on **full power** for 1 minute, then whisk in the beurre manié until smooth and thickened. Pour over the mussels, sprinkle with chopped parsley and serve.

SMOKED HADDOCK MOUSSE

Power Level: Full   **Cooking Time:** 8 Minutes
Serves 6–8

1lb (450g) smoked haddock
½ pint (300ml) milk
2oz (50g) beurre manié
   (page 44)
salt
freshly ground black pepper
½ oz (15g) packet powdered
   gelatine
2 tablespoons water

scant ½ pint (300ml) good
   thick mayonnaise
juice of 1 lemon
¼ pint (150ml) double cream,
   whipped
2 hard-boiled eggs, finely
   chopped
watercress to garnish

A more formal dish to serve for lunch with a crisp, tossed green salad and slices of granary bread and butter.

Arrange the fish in a microproof dish, cover and cook on **full power** for about 6 minutes until the flesh will flake easily. Peel off and discard skin and remove any bones. Flake the flesh.

Heat the milk in a suitable bowl for about 2 minutes, then whisk in the beurre manié until smooth and thickened. Season the sauce to taste.

Measure the gelatine into a bowl with the water and leave to stand for a few minutes to form a sponge, and then add to the hot sauce and stir until dissolved. Pour the sauce and fish into a processor or blender and purée until smooth. Leave to cool.

Add the mayonnaise and lemon juice to the sauce and fold in the whipped cream and hard-boiled eggs. Taste and check the seasoning, then pour into a 2 pint (1.2 litre) dish. Chill until firm and set.

Garnish with a few sprigs of watercress to serve.

Meat and Poultry

I have to say I had my doubts about roasting meat in the microwave. We tend to prefer it cooked in the traditional way in our house, particularly beef and pork. However, nothing venture . . .

I still cook our beef in the conventional oven (and do the Yorkshire Puddings with it), but I've given timings here for beef as well as pork in case you'd like to try them, and included a hint for rescuing crackling in the microwave on page 65. I *have* cooked lamb – especially when in a hurry – but the family still prefer it to look more 'done', not so pale, *and* they like any fat to be crisp and succulent. Don't panic if the lamb appears tough when it first comes out of the microwave. It will 'finish off', tenderize and settle on standing – for up to 20 minutes, depending on size.

Minced beef cooks beautifully – fast and with good flavour. Like lamb it's excellent for Moussaka, or for making a quick, savoury filling for taco shells. Casseroles also cook well, provided you cut the meat into even-sized cubes and keep it below the surface of the sauce or gravy as it cooks (see page 64). I cube it smaller than for conventional cooking and always buy the best quality I can. Start a casserole off on **full power**, then switch down to **low power**. The cooking time may not be shorter, but you are saving fuel.

Bacon joints need soaking first and then give excellent results, but to my mind the very best 'roaster' is chicken. The flesh stays very moist as it cooks in its own juices (especially in a roasting bag). Browning agents (such as the McCormicks and Schwarz ranges) help the appearance, but you don't get that lovely crisp skin unless you finish it off in the oven or under a hot grill. Here's a selection of my most successful recipes for you to try.

ROASTING MEATS

Always buy prime cuts of meat for microwaving; they should be roasted on no higher setting than **medium** and if a cut proves tougher than expected, braise it on **low** (or **defrost**), with extra vegetables, sliced in a little stock.

Roast meats on a microproof plastic trivet so that the cooking juices drain away and the joint doesn't boil in its own juice! Cover, during cooking, with a split roasting bag to prevent any fat from spattering inside the cooker and shield any thin parts – the end of a leg of lamb for example – by wrapping in a little foil, or it will cook before the rest of the joint.

At the end of the cooking time, wrap the meat in foil, shiny side in, and leave it to stand for 15–20 minutes, depending on the cut of the meat and the size of the joint. It will finish cooking and be easier to carve. Meat on the bone tends to cook a little quicker than a boned joint. Be guided by the cooking times on page 56.

Meat	Time on Medium power	
Beef (boned) topside, silverside sirloin	8 minutes per lb (450g) for rare 9 minutes per lb (450g) for medium 11 minutes per lb (450g) for well done	Plus 15–20 minutes of standing time before carving
Beef (on the bone) Rib	6 minutes per lb (450g) for rare 8 minutes per lb (450g) for medium 10 minutes per lb (450g) for well done	
Lamb *Pork* *Ham/Gammon*	9–12 minutes per lb (450g) 12 minutes per lb (450g) 12 minutes per lb (450g)	

These timings are for a 600-watt cooker. Allow an extra 15 seconds per minute for 400–500-watt cookers, and about 15 seconds per minute less for a 700-watt model.

COOKING WITH A BROWNING DISH OR SKILLET

Small pieces of food – chops, steaks, hamburgers, liver – which are normally grilled or fried may be cooked in the microwave on a browning skillet. You use less fat this way, but the skillet must first be preheated for about 6 minutes on **full power** – this ensures that it is hot enough to brown the food. After preheating, brush the skillet with a thin layer of oil, as this also helps the foods to brown.

Place a piece of kitchen paper over the food during cooking as this prevents the oil from spitting over the inside of the cooker. If browning larger quantities of food, simply wipe the surface of the skillet clean with another piece of kitchen paper, preheat again, this time for only 3 minutes, and brush with more oil before cooking. For more even browning, turn the food once during cooking.

BACON **Power Level:** Full **Cooking Time:** about 1 minute per rasher
Preheat the skillet for 6 minutes, coat with a little oil and

arrange the bacon on the skillet. Loosely cover with a piece of kitchen paper. Cook for 1 minute per rasher, turning after half the cooking time.

SAUSAGES   Power Level: Full   **Cooking Time:** 2 minutes per sausage
Preheat the skillet for 6 minutes, coat with a little oil and arrange the sausages on the skillet. Loosely cover with a piece of kitchen paper. Cook for 2 minutes per sausage, turning 2–3 times during cooking.

FRIED BREAD   Power Level: Full   **Cooking Time:** about 1 minute
Preheat the skillet for 6 minutes and coat with a little oil. Lightly butter the bread on both sides and arrange it on the skillet. Loosely cover with a piece of kitchen paper. Cook for 1 minute per slice, turning once during cooking.

TOASTED SANDWICHES: cook in the same way as for Fried Bread.

SUNDAY ROAST LEG OF LAMB

Power Level: Full   **Total Cooking Time:** 1 Hour 5 Minutes
Serves about 8

4lb (1.75kg) leg of lamb
a little oil for cooking
4lb (1.8kg) potatoes, par-
  boiled

3 tablespoons sweet mint
  jelly
salt
freshly ground black pepper

This is one good example of how the microwave can speed up traditional methods of cooking. The roast potatoes can start cooking in the usual oven whilst the joint is started off in the microwave and then transferred to the oven to crisp the outside.

Heat the oven to 400F (220C) gas mark 6. Put a roasting tin with a little oil in the bottom into the oven to heat through.

Lift the leg of lamb into a roasting bag and secure the end loosely with a nylon tie. Cook in the microwave on **full power** for 35 minutes, turning the joint once during cooking.

Spoon the potatoes into the roasting tin and turn them in the hot fat. Return them to the oven whilst the lamb is in the microwave. Lift the joint out of the roasting bag and into the roasting tin with the potatoes. Heat the mint jelly in a bowl for 1 minute on **full power** until melted and brush over the joint. Sprinkle with seasoning and cook in the usual oven for about 30 minutes, until the potatoes are golden and the outside of the joint is crisp. (Meanwhile, the other vegetables can be cooking in the microwave.)

ROAST SHOULDER OF LAMB

Power Level: Medium
Cooking Time: 11 Minutes per lb (450g)   **Serves 4–6**

1 shoulder of lamb, boned   microwave browning agent
  and rolled   (see below)
freshly ground black pepper

The outside of the lamb will not be brown and crisp as this cannot usually be achieved in the microwave. However, you can improve the appearance of the meat by sprinkling the outside with a little microwave browning agent. (I find McCormicks to be very good.)

Weigh the joint and calculate the cooking time, allowing 11 minutes per lb (450g). Lift the joint into a roasting bag and loosely secure the end with a nylon tie *or* stand the joint on the microproof rack of a domed microwave cooking set and cover with the dome. Cook on **medium power** for the calculated time, then lift the joint out of the roasting bag or remove the dome. Cover the meat with a piece of foil and allow to stand for 15–30 minutes, depending on the size of the joint, before carving.

Microwaving mince

Thawing is easy ... microwave 1lb (450g) frozen raw mince on **defrost** for 10 minutes. Leave to stand for 5 minutes. Complete in the usual way.

Defrost 1lb (450g) cooked mince on **full power** for 12 minutes until piping hot, stirring twice during cooking. Leave to stand for 5 minutes before serving.

IRISH STEW

Power Level: Full   **Cooking Time:** 65 Minutes
Serves 3

8oz (225g) carrots, sliced
6 pieces middle-end neck of
   lamb, trimmed of fat
2 onions, sliced
¾ pint (450ml) good light
   stock

salt
freshly ground black pepper
1lb (450g) potatoes, thinly
   sliced

Delicious and warming to serve on a cold winter's day. Use the microwave to shorten the cooking time.

Arrange the carrots in the bottom of a microproof casserole dish, then arrange the pieces of lamb on top. Arrange the slices of onion over this, pour on the stock and season well. Arrange the slices of potato on top to cover the dish completely.

Cover with a lid or pierced clear film and cook on **full power** for 20 minutes, then transfer to an oven heated to 350F (180C) gas mark 4 and cook, uncovered, for about 45 minutes until the potatoes are beginning to brown.

Pork skin

I've bought pork skin when it's on sale at my local supermarket and microwaved this for extra supplies of crackling, as the family love it. Brush with oil and sprinkle with salt. Put on an ovenglass plate lined with kitchen paper. Cover with pierced clear film and cook on **full power** for 10 minutes. Allow to stand for 2 minutes before serving.

PORK IN BRAMLEY APPLE SAUCE

Power Levels: Full and Low
Cooking Time: 68–70 Minutes   **Serves** 4

1 tablespoon sunflower oil
1 large onion, chopped
1 tablespoon flour
¾ pint (450ml) cider
1 stock cube
1½lb (750g) pork, cut into 1 inch (2.5cm) cubes
1 tablespoon apricot jam

2oz (50g) raisins
salt
freshly ground black pepper
1 small Bramley apple, peeled, cored and sliced
chopped fresh parsley to garnish

A light, fruity casserole for either fillet of pork or lean boneless pork. Good to serve in autumn when there are windfall apples about. If reheating after freezing, stir a little top of the milk into the sauce.

Measure the oil into a large bowl with the onion, stir to coat the onion with oil, then cook on **full power** for 3 minutes. Remove from the microwave, stir in the flour, then gradually blend in cider. Crumble in the stock cube, add the pork, jam, raisins and seasoning. Cover with a lid or pierced clear film then cook on **low power** for about 60 minutes, stirring once during cooking.

Add the apple and mix well, then cook on **full power** for a further 5 minutes. Turn into a warm serving dish, allow to stand for 3 minutes, then serve sprinkled with lots of freshly chopped parsley.

Serve with a baked potato and buttered carrots.

SWEET AND SOUR PORK

Power Level: Full   **Cooking Time:** 15 Minutes
Serves 3

2 teaspoons cornflour
1 tablespoon caster sugar
1 tablespoon white wine
  vinegar
2 level tablespoons tomato
  purée
1 tablespoon sherry
2 tablespoons sunflower oil
4 tablespoons pineapple juice
  from the can

12oz (350g) fillet of pork, cut
  into ½ inch (1 cm) slices
1 small green pepper, seeded
  and diced
7¾oz (220g) can pineapple
  chunks, drained
salt
freshly ground black pepper

Everything mixed together and cooked in the same bowl – so easy! Serve with plain boiled rice and perhaps a crisp green salad.

Measure the cornflour into a microproof bowl and blend in all the remaining ingredients, except the pineapple chunks. Cover with pierced clear film or a lid and cook on **full power** for 15 minutes, stirring twice during cooking. Stir in the pineapple chunks for the last 3 minutes of cooking time.

Season to taste with salt and pepper and serve with plain boiled rice.

FRUITY PORK CASSEROLE

Power Levels: Full and Low   **Cooking Time:** about 1 Hour
Serves 4

1 large onion, finely sliced
1 red pepper, cored, seeded and finely sliced
1lb (450g) pork shoulder, diced
1 clove garlic, crushed
1oz (25g) flour
2oz (50g) pre-soaked prunes

2oz (50g) pre-soaked apricots
½ teaspoon dried thyme
½ teaspoon dried marjoram
½ pint (300ml) hot stock
4oz (100g) button mushrooms
salt
freshly ground black pepper

This is a warming winter dish to serve with boiled rice (page 83) or potatoes.

Put the onion into a microproof casserole with the red pepper, cover with pierced clear film and cook on **full power** for 4 minutes. Add the pork and garlic and cook on **full power** for 4 minutes, then stir and cook for a further 3 minutes. Stir in the flour, then the prunes, apricots, herbs, stock and mushrooms and cook on **full power** for about 8 minutes, or until the stock is boiling. Season.

Cover casserole with a lid or pierced clear film and cook on **low power** for about 40 minutes, or until the meat is tender. Stir the casserole once during cooking and again at the end of cooking. Stand for 5 minutes before serving.

BOEUF BOURGUIGNONNE

Power Level: Full and Low
Cooking Time: 1 Hour 12 Minutes   **Serves 4**

1lb (450g) frying steak, cubed
4oz (100g) rindless streaky
  bacon, snipped into small
  pieces
1 tablespoon sunflower oil
1oz (25g) flour
¼ pint (150ml) good stock
½ pint (300ml) inexpensive
  red Burgundy

½ level teaspoon mixed dried
  herbs
salt
freshly ground black pepper
a dash of gravy browning
12 small pickling onions
4oz (100g) button mushrooms
chopped fresh parsley, to
  serve

*A wonderful dish for a special occasion: serve with new potatoes
and a fresh green vegetable.*

Put the steak and bacon into a microproof bowl with the oil
and mix well. Cook on **full power** for 7 minutes, stirring once
during cooking. Stir in flour, then gradually blend in the stock
and red wine. Add herbs, seasoning, gravy browning, onions
and mushrooms and mix well. Cover with pierced clear film
and cook on **full power** for 5 minutes. Stir, then cook on **low
power** for a further 60 minutes or until the meat is tender,
stirring twice during cooking.

Leave to stand for 5 minutes, then serve sprinkled with freshly
chopped parsley.

> **Tip:** when cooking casseroles, it is essential to see that
> the meat is *totally immersed* in the gravy for it to become
> tender. A saucer or small plate can be placed on the
> surface of the casserole – under the clear film – to ensure
> all the meat is covered.

BEEF OXFORD

Power Level: Full and Low   **Cooking Time:** 63–73 Minutes
Serves 4–6

2 tablespoons sunflower oil
1 large onion, chopped
1½lb (675g) good quality
  braising steak, cubed
2 cloves garlic, crushed
1oz (25g) flour

8oz (225g) mushrooms, sliced
1 large green pepper, cored,
  seeded and sliced
½ pint (300ml) hot beef stock
salt
freshly ground black pepper

Serve with plain boiled rice and a side salad.

Measure the oil into a large bowl, add the onion and cook on
full power for 3 minutes. Add the meat, garlic and flour
together with the mushrooms, pepper, stock and seasoning to
taste. Cover and cook on **full power** for 10 minutes, then
reduce the power setting to **low**. Cook for a further 50–60
minutes, or until the beef is tender, stirring from time to time.

Allow to stand for about 3 minutes before serving.

Crisp crunchy crackling

If the crackling on your roast pork isn't crunchy, try rescuing it in the microwave. Remove the scored skin – it will come off easily – brush with oil and sprinkle with salt. Put on an ovenglass plate lined with kitchen paper. Cook, uncovered, on **full power** for 30 seconds.

MEXICANO MINCE

Power Level: Full   **Cooking Time:** 18 Minutes
Serves 6

1 tablespoon sunflower oil
1 large onion, chopped
2 fat cloves garlic, crushed
1½lb (750g) good quality minced beef
1 small green pepper, cored, seeded and chopped
2oz (50g) blanched almonds, roughly chopped (optional)

2oz (50g) raisins
¾ pint (450ml) good beef stock
4 tablespoons tomato purée
1 tablespoon chilli seasoning
1 tablespoon caster sugar
salt
freshly ground black pepper

Mince cooked in the microwave is exceedingly good, but remember that you should always buy good quality lean mince, often referred to as 'ground beef' rather than 'minced beef'. This is of much higher quality and therefore better for microwave cooking.

Measure the oil, onion and garlic into a large microproof bowl or casserole. Stir to coat onion with oil, then cook on **full power** for 3 minutes. Remove from the microwave, stir in the remaining ingredients, cover with a lid or pierced clear film and cook on **full power** for 15 minutes, stirring once during cooking. Allow to stand for 3 minutes, taste to check the seasoning, then serve with plain boiled rice and a green vegetable or a tossed green salad.

Tip: stir in 4 extra tablespoons of tomato purée to make an excellent Bolognaise Sauce for pasta.

CHILLI CON CARNE

Power Level: Full   **Cooking Time:** 23 Minutes
Serves 6

4oz (100g) bacon pieces, chopped
1 onion, chopped
2 sticks celery, trimmed and sliced
1 good tablespoon flour
1½lb (675g) good quality lean minced beef
2¼oz (63g) can tomato purée

1 pint (600ml) good beef stock, heated to boiling point
2 tablespoons chilli seasoning salt
freshly ground black pepper
15oz (425g) can red kidney beans, drained
1 green pepper, cored, seeded and diced

One of the best quick mince dishes to make in the microwave: if youngsters are very hungry at lunchtime, fill pitta bread pockets with the Chilli con Carne mixture.

Measure the bacon pieces into a large microproof bowl and cook on **full power** for 3 minutes. Stir in onion and celery until evenly coated with the juices from the bacon. Cover with pierced clear film or a lid and cook on **full power** for 5 minutes. Add flour, minced beef, tomato purée, stock, chilli seasoning and salt and pepper, and mix well. Cover again and cook on **full power** for 10 minutes, stirring once during cooking. Stir in drained red kidney beans and green pepper, stir well, re-cover and cook on **full power** for 5 minutes.

Taste to check the seasoning and serve straightaway with plain boiled rice or pitta bread.

MEATBALLS IN TOMATO AND BASIL SAUCE

Power Level: Full   **Cooking Time:** 23 Minutes
Serves 4

1 large onion, chopped
1 tablespoon sunflower oil
1lb (450g) good minced beef
2oz (50g) fresh white
   breadcrumbs
salt
freshly ground black pepper
1 tablespoon freshly chopped
   parsley
1 egg, beaten

For the sauce
14oz (397g) can peeled
   tomatoes
1 tablespoon tomato purée
1 teaspoon sugar
salt
freshly ground black pepper
1 level teaspoon chopped
   basil
chopped fresh parsley, to
   serve

Delicious served with buttered noodles and a green salad. It is essential to keep rearranging the meatballs during cooking to ensure that they are all cooking evenly.

Put the onion and oil into a large but fairly shallow microproof dish and mix well. Cook on **full power** for 8 minutes, stirring once during cooking.

Measure the minced beef, breadcrumbs, seasoning, parsley and beaten egg into a mixing bowl and work together until thoroughly blended. Divide into 12 equal-size portions and, with lightly floured hands, roll into balls. Arrange meatballs on top of the onion and cook on **full power** for 2½ minutes; turn the meatballs over and rearrange in the dish, then cook for a further 2½ minutes. Again, rearrange the meatballs in the dish.

Empty the canned tomatoes into a processor or blender with the purée, sugar, seasoning and basil. Process until smooth. Spoon over the meatballs, mixing the sauce into the onion in the bottom of the dish. Cover with pierced clear film or a lid and cook on **full power** for 10 minutes.

Stir the sauce around the meatballs, allow to stand for 3 minutes and serve sprinkled with freshly chopped parsley.

MOUSSAKA

Power Levels: Full and Medium
Cooking Time: about 45 Minutes   **Serves 6**

1 large onion, chopped
1 tablespoon sunflower oil
1lb (450g) good quality mince
1oz (25g) flour
14oz (397g) can tomatoes
3½oz (142g) can tomato
   purée
¼ pint (150ml) good stock
2 level teaspoons chopped
   fresh thyme
salt
freshly ground black pepper

2 aubergines

For the sauce
¾ pint (450ml) milk
3oz (75g) beurre manié
   (page 44)
a little ground nutmeg
salt
freshly ground black pepper
6oz (175g) well-flavoured
   Cheddar cheese, grated
1 egg, beaten

The aubergines can be precooked in the microwave before being used in this dish.

Measure the onion and oil into a large microproof bowl, mix well and cook on **full power** for 3 minutes. Stir in the minced beef and flour and mix well. Gradually blend in the canned tomatoes, purée, stock, thyme and seasoning. Cover with pierced clear film or a lid and cook on **full power** for 15 minutes, stirring once during cooking.

Trim and slice the aubergines, arrange on a large microproof plate and cook on **full power** for 3 minutes. Drain well on kitchen paper.

For the sauce, heat the milk in a bowl for about 3 minutes then whisk in the beurre manié until smooth and thickened. Stir in the nutmeg, seasoning, 4oz (100g) of the cheese and the egg. Mix well.

To assemble the moussaka, layer half the meat mixture in a large ovenproof dish, cover with half the aubergines, season, then repeat the layers. Pour over the cheese sauce and sprinkle with the remaining cheese.

To serve, cook in the microwave on **full power** for 10 minutes, reduce setting to **medium power** and cook for a further 10 minutes. Brown under a hot grill.

GAMMON WITH CUMBERLAND SAUCE

Power Levels: Full and Medium
Cooking Time: 55 minutes (Gammon 30 Minutes;
Sauce 25 Minutes) **Serves 6–8**

2½lb (1.25kg) gammon joint
chopped fresh parsley, to
  serve

For the sauce
2 oranges
2 lemons

8oz (225g) redcurrant jelly
¼ pint (150ml) red wine
salt and freshly ground
  pepper
2 heaped teaspoons arrowroot
  (see recipe)
2 tablespoons cold water

Lean gammon gives very good results when cooked in the microwave.

With a very sharp knife, carefully remove the rind from the gammon joint. Lift the joint into a roasting bag. Loosely secure the end with a nylon tie and cook on **full power** for 30 minutes. Remove from the cooker and allow to cool. Lift the joint out of the roasting bag and chill well before serving as this makes carving easier. Sprinkle the top with masses of chopped parsley to serve.

For the sauce, thinly peel the rind from the oranges and lemons with a potato peeler. Cut the fruit in half and squeeze out the juice. Strain the juice into a small microproof bowl, add the redcurrant jelly and heat on **medium power** for 5 minutes, stirring once during cooking, until the jelly has melted and blended with the fruit juice. Add the red wine to the jelly, heat on **full power** for 2 minutes, then strain into a measuring jug. Season.

Shred the peel and place in a small bowl, add water to cover. Cover bowl with a lid or pierced clear film and cook on **full power** for 5 minutes. Strain, and discard the water. Cover with fresh water, cover again and cook on **full power** for a further 8 minutes, or until the peel is tender. Drain thoroughly.

For each ½ pint (300ml) sauce, blend 1 heaped teaspoon arrowroot with 1 tablespoon cold water. Stir into the sauce in the measuring jug. Cover with pierced clear film and cook on **full power** for about 5 minutes, stirring once, until the sauce is thickened. Stir in the shredded peel and pour into a serving dish.

BACON AND ONION QUICHE

Power Level: Full   **Total Cooking Time:** about 40 Minutes
Serves 6

6oz (175g) plain flour
1½oz (40g) lard
1½oz (40g) margarine
about 1½ tablespoons cold
  water

For the filling
3 eggs, beaten
½ pint (300ml) single cream

4oz (100g) well-flavoured
  Cheddar cheese, thinly
  sliced
4oz (100g) rindless streaky
  bacon, chopped
1 onion, chopped
salt
freshly ground black pepper

Using a microwave to bake pastry blind really speeds up the cooking of a quiche. Do take care not to overcook the pastry or it will become tough.

Measure the flour into a bowl and rub in the fats until the mixture resembles fine breadcrumbs. Add sufficient water to mix to a firm dough. Roll out the pastry on a lightly floured surface and use to line an 8 inch (20cm) ceramic flan dish. Prick the base well with a fork and chill in the refrigerator for about 10 minutes. Line the flan with a piece of kitchen paper and cook in the microwave on **full power** for 3½ minutes.

Whilst the flan case is still hot, brush evenly with a little of the beaten egg to seal the pastry. Stir the cream into the remaining egg. Set the conventional oven to 350F (180C) gas mark 4.

Arrange the slices of cheese in the flan case. Put the bacon into a microproof bowl and cook in the microwave on **full power** for 3 minutes; lift out with a slotted spoon and sprinkle over the cheese. Add the chopped onion to the juices left in the bowl, stir well, then cook in the microwave on **full power** for

3 minutes; add to the flan case. Season well with salt and pepper.

Pour the egg mixture over and bake in the preheated conventional oven for about 30 minutes, until the filling has set and is golden brown. Serve warm with salad.

BACON AND VEGETABLE PIE

Power Level: Full **Total Cooking Time:** about 1 Hour
Serves 4

8oz (225g) rindless streaky
  bacon, chopped
12oz (350g) raw potato, diced
12oz (350g) carrots, sliced
2 leeks, trimmed and sliced
8oz (225g) broccoli, broken
  into florets, stem chopped
1 tablespoon water
¾ pint (450ml) milk
2oz (50g) beurre manié
  (page 44)

salt
freshly ground black pepper
6oz (175g) well-flavoured
  Cheddar cheese, grated
1 teaspoon Dijon mustard
a little ground nutmeg
14oz (397g) packet frozen puff
  pastry, thawed
a little milk or beaten egg, to
  glaze

A really colourful pie which is a meal in itself: use any combination of vegetables you happen to find in the garden – or as a supermarket 'best buy'. Finish off by baking the pie in a conventional oven.

Measure the bacon into a large microproof bowl and cook on **full power** for 3 minutes. Lift out with a slotted spoon and keep on one side. Add the potato, carrot, leek, broccoli and water to the juices left in the bowl, cover with pierced clear film or a lid and cook on **full power** for 15 minutes. Add the bacon to the vegetables, mix lightly, then turn into a large pie dish.

Heat the milk in a microproof jug on **full power** for about 3 minutes, then whisk in the beurre manié until smooth and thickened. Stir in the seasoning, cheese, mustard and nutmeg and pour over the vegetables. Allow to cool. Roll out the pastry on the lightly floured surface and use to top the pie. Chill in the refrigerator until required.

To serve, heat a conventional oven to 400F (200C) gas mark 6. Brush the pie with a little milk or beaten egg and bake in the oven for about 35–40 minutes, until the pastry is well risen and golden brown. If liked, serve with a few peas.

ROASTING CHICKEN

Chicken stays moist and full of flavour when cooked in the microwave, however, it will not have its lovely crisp skin. Since my family enjoy the skin on a chicken and like it golden and crispy, I three-quarters cook the chicken in the microwave, then transfer it to the top of a very hot oven for about 15 minutes to finish cooking. However, if I am cooking the chicken to use in a different dish, or to serve in a salad, then I usually cook it totally in the microwave.

Preparing a chicken for the microwave

Stand the chicken on a microproof plastic trivet in a shallow dish, or if you have no trivet, stand it on an upturned saucer in a shallow dish. Brush with oil and season with black pepper. Cover with a slit roasting bag to cook. It may be necessary to shield the ends of the legs, the wings and breast bone with small strips of foil to prevent them overcooking.

After cooking, leave the chicken to stand, covered with foil, for at least 15 minutes before carving.

Recommended cooking times

WHOLE CHICKEN: allow 7 minutes per lb (450g) on **full power**.
CHICKEN PORTIONS: allow 6 minutes per lb (450g) on **full power**.
POUSSIN: allow 7 minutes per lb (450g) on **full power**.

To test if done
Pierce the thickest part of the thigh with a small sharp knife
and if the juices which run out are clear, then the chicken is
done. If slightly tinged with pink, the chicken should be cooked
for a little longer.

Quick 'Roast' Chicken

A microwave oven makes fast meals possible from frozen
chicken – a whole one can be defrosted in about 20
minutes. Remove giblets as soon as they are loose enough,
to speed things up. I get a lovely tender 'roast' from mine,
using a roasting bag (remember to make a slit) and
finishing it under the grill or sprinkling with a browning
agent. The skin won't be crisp.

CHICKEN WITH MADEIRA AND CREAM

Power Levels: Full, Medium and Low
Cooking Time: 48 Minutes   **Serves** 4 or 6

1 large onion, chopped
1 tablespoon sunflower oil
1 good tablespoon flour
1 tablespoon paprika pepper
½ pint (300ml) good stock, heated to boiling point
1 tablespoon tomato purée

5 tablespoons Madeira or sherry
4 chicken breasts, diced
salt
freshly ground black pepper
6oz (175g) button mushrooms, sliced
¼ pint (150ml) double cream

There is plenty of sauce with this dish so if you are serving 6, just add 2 more chicken breasts and increase the cooking time on **medium power** *to 20 minutes instead of 15 and the sauce will stretch.*

Put the onion and oil into a microproof bowl, mix well to coat the onion evenly with oil and cook on **full power** for 3 minutes. Stir in the flour and paprika until well mixed, then gradually blend in the stock. Stir in the tomato purée, Madeira, chicken and seasoning.

Cover with a lid or pierced clear film and cook on **full power** for 5 minutes, then stir and reduce power setting to **low**. Cook for 40 minutes. Add the mushrooms, stir well so thoroughly coated with sauce and cook on **medium power** for a further 5 minutes.

Stir in the cream, taste to check the seasoning, turn into a warm serving dish and serve with baby new potatoes and broccoli.

ROAST CHICKEN WITH SAGE AND APPLE SAUCE

Power Level: Full   **Cooking Time:** about 30 Minutes
Serves 6

1oz (25g) butter
1 teaspoon soy sauce
1 teaspoon Worcestershire
  sauce
a pinch of paprika pepper
3½lb (1.5kg) oven-ready
  chicken, without giblets
4–6 sprigs fresh sage
⅓ pint (200ml) cooking juices
1 teaspoon cornflour
2 tablespoons water

2 tablespoons thick natural
  yoghurt
1 egg yolk
a little chopped fresh sage
salt
freshly ground black pepper
3 green-skinned dessert
  apples
6 tablespoons redcurrant jelly
2 tablespoons water or dry
  cider

Brush the chicken with soy sauce and spices for a browner finish.

Melt the butter in a microproof jug on **full power** for 20 seconds, then stir in the soy sauce, Worcestershire sauce and paprika. Brush this over the chicken, put 3 or 4 sprigs of sage inside the cavity and place the chicken in a roasting bag. Tie loosely with a nylon tie, place in a shallow microproof dish and make 3 slits in the bag. Cook on **full power** for about 25 minutes.

Strain the cooking juices into a bowl, then wrap the chicken in foil, shiny side in, and leave to stand on a serving dish.

Stir the cornflour into the water, then add 2 tablespoons of the strained juices. Stir in the yoghurt and egg yolk, then add up to ⅓ pint (200ml) of the cooking juices. Heat on **full power** for 2 to 3 minutes, stirring twice, then season and add a little chopped fresh sage.

For the garnish, cut each apple in half across the centre. Scoop out the cores, leaving about ¾ inch (1cm) shell. Fill the centres with redcurrant jelly, then arrange in a circle in a microproof dish. Add the water or cider and cook on **full power** for 3 minutes, rearranging them halfway through. Serve with the chicken and sauce.

CURRIED CHICKEN WITH LENTILS

Power Level: Full   **Cooking Time:** about 30 Minutes
Serves 4

1 onion, finely chopped
1 tablespoon sunflower oil
2 cloves garlic, crushed
½ teaspoon mild chilli powder
½ teaspoon ground cumin
½ teaspoon turmeric
4oz (100g) green lentils

4 chicken wing portions, skinned
¾ pint (450ml) hot chicken stock
salt
freshly ground black pepper
3oz (75g) fresh spinach, shredded

If you have no fresh spinach, you can use thawed leaf spinach, provided it has been thoroughly drained. Add it to the chicken and lentils for the last few minutes of the cooking time.

Put the onion, oil and garlic into a microproof dish deep enough to take the rest of the ingredients; cover with pierced clear film and cook on **full power** for 3 minutes. Add the chilli powder, cumin and turmeric and cook on **full power** for 1 minute. Stir the mixture, then add the lentils, chicken pieces and stock. Season with salt and pepper, cover with pierced clear film or a lid and cook on **full power** for 25 minutes, stirring once during cooking.

Serve the curried chicken with a bowl of thick natural yoghurt, a crisp vegetable salad and hot, crusty wholemeal bread.

CHICKEN AND COCONUT CURRY

Power Level: Full   **Cooking Time:** 16 Minutes
Serves 4

4oz (100g) desiccated coconut
¾ pint (450ml) boiling water
4 chicken leg portions,
   skinned
2 teaspoons freshly grated
   ginger root
1½ tablespoons curry
   powder, or to taste
2 tablespoons cooking oil
1 onion, thinly sliced
1 clove garlic, crushed

3 mild green chillies, finely
   chopped
½ teaspoon *each* ground
   cumin and ground
   cardamom
¾ pint (450ml) hot chicken
   stock
salt
freshly ground black pepper
1 tablespoon desiccated or
   shredded coconut to serve

This dish reheats well if made the day before. If the sauce turns a little thin, pour it into a pan and reduce it on top of the stove until it evaporates and thickens.

Measure the coconut into a bowl and add the boiling water. Leave on one side for 30 minutes. Meanwhile, rub the chicken legs with the grated ginger and the curry powder, then heat the cooking oil in a microproof dish large enough to take the chicken and the rest of the ingredients – on **full power** for about 1 minute. Add the chicken, any remaining ginger and curry powder, then the onion, garlic, chillies and spices.

Cover with pierced clear film or a lid, then cook on **full power** for 5 minutes; turn the chicken pieces over and add stock and seasoning to taste. Cook on **full power** for a further 5 minutes. Turn and rearrange the chicken, then strain over the coconut 'milk'. Cover with pierced clear film or a lid and cook on **full power** for 5 minutes.

Lift out the chicken on to a heated serving dish, spoon over the sauce and sprinkle with extra desiccated or shredded coconut. Serve with saffron-flavoured boiled rice.

TURKEY IN CIDER AND MUSHROOM SAUCE

Power Levels: Full and Medium
Cooking Time: 70 Minutes   **Serves** 8–10

5lb (2.25kg) whole turkey
½ pint (300ml) cider
1 large onion, chopped
freshly ground black pepper

For the sauce
1 pint (600ml) milk
6oz (175g) beurre manié
  (page 44)
12oz (350g) button
  mushrooms, sliced
salt
chopped fresh parsley, to
  serve

This dish reheats very well once cooked, and may be kept in the refrigerator for up to 24 hours before serving.

Place the turkey in a microproof dish with the cider and onion and season well with pepper. Cover and cook on **medium power** for 50 minutes. Allow to stand for about an hour until cool enough to handle. To test if the turkey is done, pierce the thickest part of the thigh with a skewer. If the juices which run out are clear then the turkey is cooked; if tinged with pink, cook the turkey a little longer. Strain off the cooking liquid and skim off the fat.

Remove the meat from the turkey and cut into good-sized pieces. Heat the milk and cooking juices in a large microproof bowl on **full power** for about 5 minutes, then whisk in the beurre manié until the sauce is smooth and thickened. Add the mushrooms and seasoning to taste and stir in the turkey pieces. Turn into a serving dish.

To serve, cover with a lid or pierced clear film, and heat on **full power** for about 15 minutes. Stir twice during cooking. Serve sprinkled with lots of chopped fresh parsley.

Rice and Pasta

Cooking rice and pasta in the microwave gives excellent results, though no time is saved. The plus factors, however, are that the texture and taste are both good, there are no sticky pans to contend with – and the kitchen doesn't get hot and steamy.

It is essential to use a large bowl, since the liquid will boil up during cooking and there is nothing more irritating than having to mop up spills. I find a large ovenproof glass one works well. You can watch as it cooks. All varieties of rice cook well in the microwave and it is heaven not to have it sticking to the bottom of the pan! Any excess liquid will be absorbed by the rice during the standing time, and it will just need fluffing up with a fork to serve.

Do ensure that pasta is totally immersed in the water during cooking and if cooking long strands, such as tagliatelle or spaghetti, soften them first in boiling water to make it easier to immerse.

Cover the bowl loosely with pierced clear film or a lid during cooking, and remember to *take care* when removing the covering after cooking. It will release a cloud of scalding steam so remove film from the side of the bowl furthest away from you first to allow the gush of steam to escape.

I find it best when cooking a pasta dish such as Spaghetti Bolognaise, to cook the spaghetti conventionally in a pan of boiling salted water and whilst this is cooking, reheat the spaghetti sauce in the microwave so that both are ready to serve at the same time.

PLAIN BOILED RICE

Power Level: Full   **Cooking Time:** 15 Minutes
Serves 3

8oz (225g) long grain rice
scant 1 pint (600ml) water,
    heated to boiling point
salt

*This works well, doesn't boil dry and every grain stays separate.
I found Uncle Ben's rice best.*

Measure the rice, water and salt into a large ovenproof glass
bowl, stir well. Cover with pierced clear film. Cook on **full
power** for 15 minutes, then remove from oven and leave to
stand for 5 minutes until the water is absorbed. Fluff up the
grains with a fork and serve.

CHICKEN RISOTTO

Power Level: Full   **Cooking Time:** 30 Minutes
Serves 4

1 large onion, chopped
2 cloves garlic, crushed
1 red pepper, cored, seeded
  and diced
2 tablespoons sunflower oil
4 chicken breasts, diced
8oz (225g) long grain rice
scant 1 pint (600ml) good
  stock, heated to boiling
  point

salt
freshly ground black pepper
3 tomatoes, skinned and
  quartered
4oz (100g) button
  mushrooms, sliced
2 tablespoons chopped fresh
  parsley

This dish may not be speedier to cook, but it tastes very good!

Measure the onion, garlic, red pepper and oil into a large microproof bowl and mix well. Cook on **full power** for 5 minutes. Stir in the chicken breasts, rice, stock and seasoning. Cover with pierced clear film and cook on **full power** for 20 minutes, stirring twice during cooking. Mix in the tomatoes and mushrooms and cook on **full power** for a further 5 minutes.

Stir in the parsley and allow to stand for 2 minutes before serving.

SAVOURY VEGETABLE RICE

Power Level: Full   **Cooking Time:** 32 Minutes
Serves 4

2 tablespoons sunflower oil
1 large onion, chopped
1 red pepper, cored, seeded
  and diced
1 large carrot, diced
1 clove garlic, crushed
8oz (225g) broccoli, cut into
  ½ inch (1cm) pieces

8oz (225g) long grain rice
1 pint (600ml) chicken stock
salt
freshly ground black pepper
8oz (225g) frozen peas
2 tablespoons chopped fresh
  parsley

Can be served either as a vegetable dish with meats, or as a satisfying meal in itself. Sprinkle with a little grated cheese.

Measure the oil into a large microproof bowl with the onion, pepper, carrot and garlic. Mix well and cook on **full power** for 7 minutes. Stir in all the remaining ingredients except the peas and parsley. Stir well, cover with pierced clear film and cook on **full power** for 15 minutes. Add the peas, stir, re-cover and cook for a further 10 minutes.

Allow to stand for about 5 minutes, then fork in the parsley and serve hot.

SMOKED HADDOCK WITH RIBBON NOODLES

Power Level: Full   **Cooking Time:** 19 Minutes
Serves 4

8oz (225g) ribbon noodles
1lb (450g) smoked haddock
    fillets
2oz (50g) butter
1 onion, chopped
1 good tablespoon flour

1 pint (600ml) milk
salt
freshly ground black pepper
4oz (100g) well-flavoured
    Cheddar cheese, grated

I prefer my pasta cooked in the traditional way in plenty of boiling salted water, so I save time by using the microwave to cook the fish and sauce while the noodles are cooking.

Cook the noodles in plenty of boiling salted water as directed on the packet. Drain and rinse well.

Whilst the noodles are cooking, arrange the fish fillets on a large, microproof plate, cover with pierced clear film and cook on **full power** for 5 minutes.

Measure the butter into a large microproof bowl and heat on **full power** for 1 minute until melted. Add onion, mix well and cook on **full power** for 5 minutes. Meanwhile, skin and flake the fish.

Stir in the flour and gradually blend in the milk. Cover with a lid or pierced clear film and cook on **full power** for 8 minutes, stirring once during cooking and again at the end of the cooking time.

Stir in the drained noodles and skinned and flaked fish. Season to taste, then turn into a warmed flameproof serving dish. Sprinkle with cheese and brown under a hot grill until the cheese has melted and is golden brown. Serve straightaway.

ITALIAN TUNA SAUCE WITH PASTA

Power Level: Full   **Cooking Time:** 18 Minutes
Serves 4

8oz (225g) pasta shells
1½oz (40g) butter
4oz (100g) button
    mushrooms, sliced
1½oz (40g) flour
1 pint (600ml) milk
salt
freshly ground black pepper

2 × 7oz (198g) cans tuna fish,
    drained
4 hard-boiled eggs, quartered
4oz (100g) well-flavoured
    Cheddar cheese, grated
a little freshly chopped
    parsley, to serve

*This tuna sauce can be served with any type of pasta. I have
chosen shells for this recipe, but tagliatelle, macaroni and
spaghetti all work equally well.*

Cook the pasta shells in a large pan of boiling water until just
tender. Drain and rinse well.

For the sauce, measure the butter into a microproof bowl and
heat on **full power** for 1 minute. Stir in the mushrooms and
cook on **full power** for 1 minute, then stir in the flour and
gradually blend in the milk. Heat on **full power** for 6 minutes,
stirring once during cooking and again at the end of the
cooking time to give a thickened sauce. Stir in the seasoning,
tuna, eggs and cooked pasta shells and toss lightly until evenly
coated with sauce.

Turn into a flameproof serving dish, sprinkle with cheese and
heat on **full power** for 10 minutes until heated through, then
brown under a hot grill until the cheese is golden. Sprinkle
with parsley and serve hot with a tomato salad.

Tagliatelle al Tonno

For an extra-quick variation, cook the chopped onion in 2 tablespoons olive oil on **full power** for 3 minutes. Stir in the flaked tuna fish with the mushrooms and cook on **full power** for 4–5 minutes, stirring twice, until heated through and the mushrooms are cooked. Season to taste, add up to ¼ pint (150ml) whipping cream and reheat on **low power**. Serve with cooked tagliatelle.

LASAGNE

Power Level: Full   **Cooking Time:** about 1 Hour
Serves 6

5oz (150g) Barilla lasagne

For the meat sauce
1 tablespoon sunflower oil
1lb (450g) minced beef
1oz (25g) rindless streaky
  bacon, chopped
8oz (225g) onion, chopped
4 sticks celery, chopped
½oz (15g) flour
½ pint (300ml) stock
3½oz (90g) can tomato purée
2 cloves garlic, crushed
salt and freshly ground
  pepper

2 teaspoons soft brown sugar
¼ teaspoon dried mixed
  herbs

For the white sauce
1 pint (600ml) milk
3oz (75g) beurre manié
  (page 44)
salt
freshly ground black pepper
a little ground nutmeg
½ teaspoon Dijon mustard
8oz (225g) well-flavoured
  Cheddar cheese, grated

Use Barilla lasagne for this recipe since it needs no precooking.

For the meat sauce, measure the oil, beef and bacon into a bowl; mix lightly. Cover with a lid or pierced clear film and cook on **full power** for 5 minutes. Add onion and celery and

Overleaf: Dry Crunchy Muesli with fresh fruit
Above: Poached Salmon with a strawberry and
cucumber salad and Hollandaise Sauce
Right: Fruity Pork Casserole served with
Plain Boiled Rice

Left: Chicken and Coconut Curry
served with saffron rice
Above: Tagliatelle al Tonno

Above: Butterscotch Fudge Cake
Right: Soft Fruit Flan with Chilled
Blackcurrant Creams and Blackberry Mousse
Overleaf: Tomato Chutney, Rhubarb and Raisin Chutney,
and Apple and Molasses Chutney

cook on **full power** for a further 5 minutes. Stir in the flour and remaining meat sauce ingredients, mix well, re-cover and cook on **full power** for 20 minutes, stirring twice during cooking.

For the white sauce, heat the milk in a jug on **full power** for about 4 minutes; whisk in the beurre manié until smooth and thickened. Stir in the seasonings.

In a shallow flameproof serving dish, about 3½ pint (2 litre) capacity, put a third of the meat sauce, then a third of the white sauce and a third of the cheese, followed by half the lasagne. Repeat the layers, add the remaining meat sauce and white sauce, finishing with cheese. Leave until cold.

To serve, cook in the microwave on **full power** for 15 minutes, then transfer to a hot grill until the cheese is golden brown and bubbling. Serve at once.

Vegetable Dishes

Most vegetables cook beautifully in the microwave, retaining their fresh, full flavour, bright colour, crispness and shape. You need just a very little water. I give all the basic cooking instructions and timing in the form of charts beginning on page 93. Never add seasoning until after cooking, and don't sprinkle salt directly on to the vegetables before cooking as this causes dehydrated patches to form on the top.

Always cover vegetables during cooking and remember to puncture the clear film, or turn back a corner, to allow steam to escape. Frozen vegetables can be cooked straightaway from frozen – just snip a corner of the bag and place it on a microproof plate. Any leftover vegetables can be reheated and taste just as fresh, or toss them in a dressing and serve as a salad. Otherwise, I put them into cheese or egg dishes with a sauce for a quick family lunch dish.

It's most important to remember to prick the skins of potatoes – or anything else you cook 'in its skin' – otherwise they'll burst during cooking. You'll only forget once, I promise you! And remember that vegetables continue to cook once they are taken out of the microwave. So do allow for standing time (it's in the charts) rather than being tempted to cook them that little bit longer, if they don't feel cooked when you first take them out.

If you are cooking a mixture of vegetables in the same container, arrange the ones that take the longest cooking time (usually root vegetables) on the outside in a ring, and the ones that cook in less time (most green vegetables) towards the centre of the dish. I find it a great help, when entertaining, to arrange a plate of part-cooked vegetables on a serving platter well ahead of a dinner party, then I reheat them for a few minutes in the microwave before serving. It certainly makes it all much easier – and the vegetables taste so good!

GUIDE TO COOKING FRESH VEGETABLES

For small, very young vegetables reduce the cooking time slightly.

Vegetables	Quantity	Preparation	Cooking Time Minutes on Full Power	Standing Time Minutes
Artichoke, Globe	1 2 4	Discard tough outer leaves. Snip tips of leaves with scissors. Cut off stem. Cook with ¼ pint (150ml) water in covered dish. Check after minimum time. Leaf can be pulled away easily when cooked. Drain upside down and serve.	5–6 7–8 12–14	3–5 3–5 5
Artichoke, Jerusalem	1lb/450g	Trim. Peel and cube. Put in a dish with 6 tablespoons water. Cover to cook. Stir once during cooking.	8–10	3
Asparagus	1lb/450g	Trim stalks if necessary. Arrange in dish with thick stalk to outside and tender tip to centre. Add 5 tablespoons water. Cover to cook. Rearrange once during cooking.	6–8	3
Aubergines	1 whole	Trim and slice. Arrange in 1 layer in dish. Add 2 tablespoons water and cover to cook. Stir once during cooking.	4–6	3
Beans, Broad	1lb/450g shelled weight	Place in dish, add 4 tablespoons water. Cover to cook. Stir once during cooking.	8	5

Vegetables	Quantity	Preparation	Cooking Time Minutes on Full Power	Standing Time Minutes
Beans, Whole French	1lb/450g	Top and tail. Place in dish, add 4 tablespoons water. Cover to cook.	7	5
Beans, Runner	1lb/450g	Top, tail and string. Slice. Put in dish with 4 tablespoons water. Cover to cook. Stir once during cooking.	6	3
Beetroot	1lb/450g	Choose small beetroot. Twist off leaves leaving 1 inch (2.5cm) stalk. Put in dish with ¼ pint (150ml) water. Cover to cook. Turn once during cooking. Allow to cool slightly, then peel.	20–25	10
Broccoli and Calabrese	1lb/450g	Remove outer leaves, trim off any woody stem. Arrange in dish with stalks to outside and florets towards the centre. Add 4 tablespoons water. Cover to cook. Rearrange once during cooking.	6–8	3–5
Brussels Sprouts	1lb/450g	Trim and cut a cross in the base. Put in dish. Add 4 tablespoons water. Cover to cook. Stir once during cooking.	7–8	3–5
Cabbage	1lb/450g	Trim outside leaves. Shred coarsely. Put in large dish with ¼ pint (150ml) water. Cover to cook. Drain before serving.	8–10	3
Carrots	1lb/450g	Peel and slice or dice larger ones. Small baby carrots need a shorter cooking time. Put in dish, add 4 tablespoons water. Cover to cook. Stir once during cooking.	6–8	5
Cauliflower	1 whole	Trim outer leaves, cut a cross in the base. Put stem side uppermost in deep dish. Add ¼ pint (150ml) water. Cover to cook.	10–12	5
	1lb/450g	Break into florets. Put in dish, add 6 tablespoons water. Cover to cook. Stir once during cooking.	7–10	3

Vegetables	Quantity	Preparation	Cooking Time Minutes on Full Power	Standing Time Minutes
Celery	1lb/450g	Slice or leave whole. Put in dish, add 4 tablespoons water or stock. Cover to cook. Rearrange once during cooking.	12–15	5
Celeriac	1lb/450g	Peel and dice. Put in dish, add 6 tablespoons water. Cover to cook. Stir once during cooking. Mash with butter, salt and pepper.	8–10	5
Chicory	4 whole	Trim. Arrange in dish, add 4 tablespoons water. Cover to cook. Rearrange once during cooking.	5–8	3
Corn on the Cob	2 whole	Remove husks and silks. Arrange in dish, add 3 tablespoons water. Cover to cook. Rearrange once during cooking.	6–8	3–5
Courgettes	1lb/450g	Slice into 1 inch (2.5cm) rounds. Add 1oz (25g) butter. Cover to cook. Stir once during cooking.	5–6	5
Fennel	2 heads	Trim, cut into slices. Arrange in shallow dish, add 4 tablespoons water. Cover to cook. Stir once during cooking.	6–8	5
Leeks	1lb/450g	Wash thoroughly. If young leave whole, otherwise slice into even rounds. Place in dish, add 4 tablespoons water. Cover to cook. Rearrange once during cooking.	10–12	3
Marrow	1lb/450g	Peel and slice. Arrange in dish, add 2oz (50g) butter. Cover to cook. Rearrange once during cooking.	8	5
Mushrooms	8oz/225g	Leave small button mushrooms whole; slice larger ones. Put in dish, add 1oz (25g) butter. Cover to cook. Rearrange once during cooking.	3–4	3

Vegetables	Quantity	Preparation	Cooking Time Minutes on Full Power	Standing Time Minutes
Mangetout	1lb/450g	Top and tail and string, if necessary. Place in dish, add 1oz (25g) butter. Cover to cook. Rearrange once during cooking.	5–6	5
Onions	4 medium	Peel and leave whole or quarter. Place in dish, add 4 tablespoons water. Cover to cook. Rearrange once during cooking.	10	3
Parsnips	1lb/450g	Trim, peel and cube. Put in dish with 6 tablespoons water. Cover to cook. Stir once during cooking.	8–10	3
Peas	1lb/450g	Shell. Put in a dish with 4 tablespoons water. Cover to cook. Stir once during cooking.	6–8	5
Potatoes	1lb/450g	Peel and quarter. Place in a dish with 6 tablespoons water. Cover to cook. Rearrange once during cooking.	10–12	5
Spinach	1lb/450g	Wash. Place in roasting bag, loosely tie end with string or plastic tie. Drain if necessary after cooking.	6	3
Swede	1lb/450g	Peel, cube. Place in a dish with 6 tablespoons water. Cover to cook. Stir twice during cooking.	10–13	3–5
Tomatoes	2	Halve. Arrange in a dish, top with a small knob of butter and pepper. Cover to cook.	1–2	2
Turnips	1lb/450g	Peel. Cube. Place in a dish with 6 tablespoons water. Cover to cook. Stir twice during cooking.	10–13	3–5

Vegetables should only be seasoned with salt at the end of cooking.

GUIDE TO COOKING FROZEN VEGETABLES

Vegetable	Quantity	Cooking Time Minutes on Full Power	Standing Time Minutes
Asparagus	1lb/450g	11	3
Beans, Broad	1lb/450g	10	3
Beans, French or Runner	1lb/450g	11	3
Broccoli	1lb/450g	6–8	3
Cabbage	1lb/450g	10	5
Carrots	1lb/450g	10–12	5
Cauliflower	1lb/450g	8–10	3
Corn on the Cob	1lb/450g	6–8	3
Courgettes	1lb/450g	6	3
Diced Mixed Vegetables	1lb/450g	7	5
Mangetout	1lb/450g	6	3
Peas	1lb/450g	6	3
Root Vegetables	1lb/450g	10–12	5
Spinach	1lb/450g	10	3
Turnip	1lb/450g	10–12	5

IN THE BAG

Frozen vegetables are very successfully defrosted or reheated in the microwave. On the whole, it is not necessary to add any extra water for cooking. Small bags of vegetables can be reheated in the bags in which they were bought or frozen. Just place them on a plate for support and remove any ties. Bought bags of frozen vegetables just need the corner of the bag snipping with scissors before cooking.

'LOOSE' VEGETABLES

Otherwise, put the vegetable into a dish and cover before cooking. The cooking times above are average, so your own personal preference must be taken into account and the cooking time calculated accordingly. Add a few more minutes if you prefer the vegetables more tender, but do remember also to allow for them to finish cooking during **standing time**. For crisper vegetables, reduce the cooking time slightly.

BLANCHING VEGETABLES FOR THE FREEZER

Blanching vegetables in the microwave could not be simpler:

no need for pans of boiling water and hot, steamy kitchens. It is perfect for home-grown produce since the vegetables can be picked and ready to freeze in a matter of minutes, ensuring that none of the freshness is lost.

The vegetables can be blanched in boil-in or freezer bags. Prepare the vegetables as you would do normally, place in the bag with 3–6 tablespoons of water (see below), blanch, and whilst still in the bag, plunge straight into icy water. This chills the vegetables quickly and expels air from the bag, giving a 'vacuum pack' which is ready for freezing. Seal and label as usual and freeze.

GUIDE TO BLANCHING FRESH VEGETABLES

Vegetable	Quantity	Amount of Water in Tablespoons	Time in Minutes on Full Power
Asparagus	1lb/450g	3	3–4
Beans	1lb/450g	5	6
Broccoli	1lb/450g	4	5
Brussels Sprouts	1lb/450g	6	4–6
Carrots	1lb/450g	3	4
Cauliflower	1lb/450g	5	4–5
Corn on the Cob	1lb/450g	3	6
Courgettes	1lb/450g	3	3
Leeks	1lb/450g	3	6
Onions	4 medium, quartered	4	4–5
Parsnips	1lb/450g	3	3–4
Peas	1lb/450g	3	4–6
Spinach	1lb/450g	–	4

To dry herbs

Leafy herbs such as parsley, tarragon and sage work best: sandwich the herbs between two sheets of kitchen paper and heat on **full power** for 1 to 3 minutes or until dry and crumbly. Check frequently, as the timing will vary with the type of herb. Put a cup of water in the microwave when heating the herbs.

BAKED POTATOES

Potatoes bake well in the microwave especially if you are in a hurry, but they don't have that lovely crisp skin you get when they are in the conventional oven. I often start the potatoes in the microwave, then transfer them to a very hot oven for about 15 minutes to crisp the skins, since that is how my family prefers them.

Prick the potatoes with a fork to prevent them bursting during cooking and calculate the cooking time according. Do leave the potatoes **to stand** for a good 5–10 minutes before serving as this will give sufficient time for the residual heat to cook them right through to the centre. If they still feel crisp when they first come out of the cooker, don't be tempted to put them back for a little longer; they would only start cooking from the outside again.

Cooking times

1 large potato: 8 minutes on **full power** plus 5 minutes standing time.
2 large potatoes: 16 minutes on **full power** plus 7 minutes standing time.
4 large potatoes: 30 minutes on **full power** plus 10 minutes standing time.

For smaller potatoes, reduce the cooking time slightly.

TOPPINGS FOR 2 LARGE POTATOES

Cheese and Ham Scoop out the insides of the potatoes and mix well with 2oz (50g) well-flavoured Cheddar cheese, 2oz (50g) chopped ham and 1 teaspoon Dijon mustard. Season, then spoon back into potato shells; reheat on **full power** for about 4 minutes.

Cream Cheese and Chive Scoop out the insides of the potatoes and mix with 3oz (75g) cream cheese, 1 tablespoon freshly snipped chives, a crushed clove of garlic and 2 tablespoons of the top of the milk. Season to taste, spoon back into the potato shells and reheat on **full power** for about 4 minutes.

Tomato and Onion Scoop out the middle of the potatoes and mix with 2 skinned and chopped tomatoes and 2oz (50g) cooked onion. Season to taste, then spoon back into the potato shells and reheat on **full power** for about 4 minutes.

POTATO DAUPHINOISE

Power Level: Full   **Cooking Time:** 14 Minutes
Serves 3

1oz (25g) butter
1lb (450g) potatoes
salt
freshly ground black pepper

½ teaspoon nutmeg
5 tablespoons single cream
2oz (50g) Gruyère cheese, grated

This is a wonderful dish for entertaining as it can be part-cooked ahead – which prevents the potatoes going black. Then it can be slipped into a hot conventional oven to brown the cheese and crispen the edges. Alternatively, if serving straight-away, it can be browned under the grill.

Measure the butter into a 7 inch (17.5cm) round shallow microproof serving dish and heat it in the microwave for 1 minute, or until the butter is melted. Slice the potatoes *very* thinly (by hand or in a processor) and arrange them in layers in the buttered dish. Season with salt and pepper between the layers. Sprinkle the nutmeg on top, cover with pierced clear film and cook on **full power** for 10 minutes.

Pour the single cream over the potatoes and sprinkle the grated cheese on top. Cook on **full power** for 2 minutes, or until the cheese has melted. Brown under a hot grill for 2 minutes.

LAYERED POTATO AND CELERIAC

Power Level: Full   **Cooking Time:** 15 Minutes
Serves 4

1lb (450g) potatoes
1lb (450g) celeriac
a knob of butter
¼ pint (150ml) stock

salt
freshly ground black pepper
freshly chopped parsley, to
serve

Celeriac is becoming more and more popular; it has a wonderful flavour and goes particularly well with potatoes.

Finely slice the potatoes and celeriac and arrange in alternate layers in a lightly buttered microproof dish, seasoning well between the layers and finishing with a layer of potato. Pour over the stock. Cover with pierced clear film or a lid and cook on **full power** for 15 minutes, then transfer to a hot grill to brown the top layer of potato. Serve sprinkled with chopped parsley.

Softening butter or soft cheese
Butter or full-fat soft cheese creams more easily if softened first for 15 to 30 seconds on **medium power**.

VEGETABLE PURÉES

These are very popular now, and I like to serve a party selection arranged on a platter in a cartwheel effect. Prepare them ahead of the party and arrange on the serving dish. Cover with clear film, then pierce the top and reheat in the microwave for about 6 minutes on **full power** when required. Allow 6oz (175g) vegetables per person.

CELERIAC PURÉE
Cook equal quantities of celeriac and potato until tender (see Charts on pages 93–6). Drain, then mash to a purée. Season to taste with salt and freshly ground black pepper, and serve topped with a knob of butter.

SPROUT PURÉE
Cook the sprouts until tender. Drain well, then transfer to a processor or blender and reduce to a purée with a little single cream, salt and freshly ground black pepper.

SWEDE PURÉE
Prepare the swede and cook until tender. Drain well, then mash with a potato masher until smooth. Season well with salt and freshly ground black pepper, and stir in a little single cream.

CURRIED PARSNIP PURÉE
Cook the parsnips until tender. Drain well, then mash until smooth. Season with salt, freshly ground black pepper, ½ level teaspoon curry powder and a little single cream.

BRAISED CELERY

Power Level: Full   **Cooking Time:** 10 Minutes
Serves 4–6

1 head celery
1lb (450g) onions, sliced
salt
freshly ground black pepper

1 pint (600ml) chicken stock
freshly chopped parsley, to
serve

I often prepare this when celery heads are being sold cheaply at the supermarket.

Wash the celery and cut into 3 inch (7.5cm) lengths. Arrange in alternate layers in a dish with the onion. Season well, then pour over the stock.

Cover with pierced clear film, and cook on **full power** for 10 minutes. Allow to stand for 5 minutes and serve sprinkled with lots of freshly chopped parsley.

LEEKS IN CIDER SAUCE

Power Level: Full   **Cooking Time:** 10 Minutes
Serves 4

1lb (450g) leeks
¼ pint (150ml) cider
salt
freshly ground black pepper

1oz (25g) beurre manié
(page 44)
freshly chopped parsley, to
serve

These go particularly well with roast lamb or hot cooked ham.

Trim the leeks and cut them into 2 inch (5cm) lengths. Arrange in a shallow microproof dish, pour the cider over, sprinkle with a little seasoning and cover with pierced clear film or a lid and cook on **full power** for 10 minutes, turning the leeks over once during cooking. Stir in the beurre manié until well mixed and slightly thickened. Sprinkle with lots of freshly chopped parsley to serve.

CABBAGE AU GRATIN

Power Level: Full   **Cooking Time:** 15 Minutes
Serves 3

½ pint (300ml) milk
2oz (50g) beurre manié
  (page 44)
salt
freshly ground black pepper
a little ground nutmeg
½ teaspoon Dijon mustard

12oz (350g) cabbage,
  shredded
¼ pint (150ml) water
2oz (50g) well-flavoured
  Cheddar cheese, grated
1oz (25g) fresh white
  breadcrumbs

This transforms the humble cabbage into a dish good enough for a dinner party!

Heat the milk in a microproof bowl on **full power** for about 2 minutes, then whisk in the beurre manié until smooth and thickened. Add seasoning to taste, nutmeg and mustard. Put the cabbage in a bowl with the water, cover with pierced clear film and cook on **full power** for 6 minutes. Drain thoroughly then stir into the sauce. Turn into a flameproof serving dish and sprinkle with cheese and breadcrumbs.

To serve, heat the dish on **full power** for 7 minutes, then transfer to a hot grill until the cheese and breadcrumbs are golden brown.

BAKED PARSNIPS & CHEESY TOPPING

Power Level: Full **Cooking Time:** 11 Minutes
Serves 2

1 tablespoon sunflower oil
1lb (450g) parsnips, diced
8oz (225g) ham, chopped
8oz (225g) can tomatoes
1 tablespoon freshly chopped
  parsley

salt
freshly ground black pepper
2oz (50g) fresh white
  breadcrumbs
2oz (50g) well-flavoured
  Cheddar cheese, grated

*Serve hot with crisp French bread as a light lunch or supper
dish.*

Measure the oil into a shallow microproof dish with the
parsnip and mix lightly. Cover with pierced clear film and
cook on **full power** for 3 minutes. Stir in the ham. Pour on the
canned tomatoes, sprinkle with parsley and season well.

Mix the breadcrumbs and cheese together and sprinkle over
the parsnips. Cook on **full power** for 8 minutes, then transfer
to a hot grill until the cheese and breadcrumbs are golden
brown. Serve straightaway.

AUTUMN VEGETABLE CASSEROLE

Power Level: Full   **Cooking Time:** 10 Minutes
Serves 6

1 medium aubergine,
   trimmed and thinly sliced
1 green pepper, cored, seeded
   and cut into strips
1 red pepper, cored, seeded
   and cut into strips
2 medium onions, chopped
4 tablespoons sunflower oil

1lb (450g) courgettes, sliced
6 large tomatoes, skinned
   and quartered
salt
freshly ground black pepper
2 tablespoons freshly chopped
   parsley (optional)
juice of ½ lemon

If you like crisp vegetables, cook for less time. Use yellow peppers, too, for a change.

Arrange aubergine slices on a large microproof plate and cook on **full power** for 3 minutes. Set aside.

Put the green pepper, red pepper and onion into a bowl with the oil and mix well, so the vegetables are thoroughly coated with oil. Cover with pierced clear film and cook on **full power** for 5 minutes. Stir in the courgettes, aubergines and tomatoes until thoroughly mixed, then cook on **full power** for a further 5 minutes.

Remove from the microwave, stir in seasoning to taste, add parsley and lemon juice. Allow to stand for 2 minutes before serving.

SUMMER VEGETABLES IN MILD CURRIED SAUCE

Power Level: Full   **Cooking Time:** 15–18 Minutes
Serves 3–4

2 tablespoons sunflower oil
1 large onion, chopped
2 sticks celery, sliced
2 courgettes, sliced
8oz (225g) cauliflower,
  broken into florets
4oz (100g) button
  mushrooms, sliced

3 tomatoes, skinned and
  quartered
salt
freshly ground black pepper
1oz (25g) flour
1 level teaspoon curry powder
½ pint (300ml) good stock
1 level tablespoon redcurrant
  jelly

A perfect dish for vegetarians; it is also good as an accompaniment to chops or grilled meat. Serve with rice or noodles to mop up the sauce.

Measure the oil into a large microproof bowl with the onion and cook on **full power** for 3 minutes. Stir in the remaining vegetables and seasoning. Blend the flour and curry powder with a little of the stock to give a smooth paste. Blend in the remaining stock, then pour over the vegetables and add the redcurrant jelly. Stir well.

Cover with pierced clear film and cook on **full power** for 12–15 minutes, stirring twice during cooking and again at the end of cooking. Allow to stand for 5 minutes before serving.

Quick Sauces

There's really no excuse for even the most nervous of cooks to avoid sauce-making any longer. The microwave really does make it all so easy! The joy is that they need so little attention during cooking, and as they are not made in anything metal, there's very little likelihood of a scorched pan to contend with afterwards. I have found that even the richest of sauces – those thickened with eggs or cream (like a Hollandaise or a Crème Caramel) – will not curdle as long as they are cooked on **low power** for no longer than the necessary time (that is, until thick). Many sauces tend to thicken a little on standing.

The only real art in making your sauces in the microwave is to give them a really good whisk – especially if they are thickened with flour, although you'll find my beurre manié method helps to keep out the lumps. Don't use a metal whisk though. I use one of those plastic balloon types that you can buy very cheaply from a cookshop or microwave equipment suppliers.

Choose a jug or bowl which is large enough to prevent the sauce from boiling over as milk tends to rise rather quickly! It should have room enough for you to give the sauce a good whisk at the end of cooking, too.

Microwaved Bread Sauce is very good – fluffy and thick – and for good measure, I have included my favourite Spaghetti Sauce. And no sauce chapter would be complete without a Chocolate Sauce for the children.

MAKING GRAVY

Whether using instant gravy powder or making gravy in the traditional way, the microwaved results are lump-free! It is essential, however, to give the gravy a good whisk at the end of cooking.

TRADITIONAL GRAVY

Pour off most of the fat from the roasting tin, leaving about 2 tablespoons of the sediment. Stir in 1 level tablespoon plain flour and blend thoroughly with the fat. Gradually blend in ½ pint (300ml) hot stock. Transfer to a large microproof jug or bowl and heat on **full power** for 2½–3 minutes, whisking once during cooking and again at the end of the cooking time. Add seasoning to taste and serve.

INSTANT GRAVY

Blend 3 teaspoons instant gravy powder with a little water in a large microproof jug or bowl. Gradually blend in ½ pint (300ml) hot stock. Heat on **full power** for 2½–3 minutes, whisking well once during cooking and again at the end of cooking. Taste for seasoning and serve.

BASIC WHITE SAUCE

Power Level: Full   **Cooking Time:** 2–3 Minutes

½ pint (300ml) milk   salt
2oz (50g) beurre manié   freshly ground black pepper
  (page 44)

*Very simple: made and served in the same jug . . . Don't leave a
wire whisk in the bowl when the bowl's in the microwave,
though.*

Heat the milk in a jug on **full power** for 2 to 3 minutes, then
whisk in the beurre manié until the sauce is smooth and
thickened. Add seasoning to taste and serve or use as a base
for other sauces or dishes.

CHEESE SAUCE: add 3oz (75g) well-flavoured grated Cheddar
cheese, 1 teaspoon Dijon mustard and a little freshly ground
nutmeg to the Basic White Sauce. Mix well and heat on **full
power** for 1 minute before serving.

PARSLEY SAUCE: add 1 tablespoon chopped fresh parsley to the
Basic White Sauce. Mix well and heat on **full power** for 1
minute before serving.

MUSHROOM SAUCE: add 3oz (75g) finely sliced mushrooms to
the sauce. Mix well and cook on **full power** for about 2
minutes until the mushrooms are tender before serving.

MUSTARD SAUCE: stir 1½–2 tablespoons made English mustard
blended with 1 tablespoon white wine vinegar and 2 teaspoons
sugar into the Basic White Sauce. Heat on **full power** for 1
minute until piping hot before serving.

BREAD SAUCE

Power Level: Medium   **Cooking Time:** 14 Minutes
Serves 6

1 onion, peeled
2 cloves
1 pint (600ml) milk
3oz (75g) white breadcrumbs

salt
freshly ground black pepper
a knob of butter

Serve with chicken and turkey. The bread sauce can be kept warm in the microwave on the **low** *or* **defrost power** *settings, but do cover it with a damp piece of greaseproof paper to prevent a skin from forming.*

Stick the cloves into the onion, place in a microproof bowl with the milk. Heat on **medium power** for 8 minutes, then leave to stand for 30 minutes. Lift out the onion and stir in the breadcrumbs, seasoning and butter. Turn into a microproof serving dish, reheat on **medium power** for about 6 minutes until heated through, then cover with damp greaseproof paper and keep warm until required.

APPLE SAUCE

Power Level: Medium   **Cooking Time:** 8–10 Minutes
Serves 6

1lb (450g) cooking apples
5 tablespoons water
juice of ½ a lemon

1oz (25g) butter
sugar to taste

Delicious served with duck, goose or pork.

Peel, core and slice the apples. Place them in a microproof bowl with the water and lemon juice. Cover with pierced clear film or a lid and cook on **medium power** for 8–10 minutes until the apples are soft, stirring once during cooking. Beat well with a wooden spoon until smooth. Add the butter and sugar to taste.

RICH ONION SAUCE

Power Level: Full   **Cooking Time:** 15 Minutes
Serves 4–6

2 tablespoons sunflower oil
1 large onion, finely chopped
2oz (50g) flour
1 pint (600ml) hot stock
3 tablespoons tomato ketchup

a few drops of Worcestershire
  sauce
¼ level teaspoon dried
  marjoram
salt
freshly ground black pepper

Serve with liver, meatballs, meat loaf or beefburgers.

Measure the oil and onion into a microproof bowl and cook on **full power** for 5 minutes until the onion has softened. Stir in the flour and gradually blend in the stock. Add the tomato ketchup, Worcestershire sauce and marjoram. Season to taste and mix well. Cover with pierced clear film and cook on **full power** for up to 10 minutes, beating well twice during cooking and once again thoroughly at the end of cooking.

QUICK PROVENÇAL SAUCE

Power Level: Full   **Cooking Time:** 11 Minutes
Serves 4

2 tablespoons sunflower oil
1 large onion, chopped
1 fat clove garlic, crushed
14oz (397g) can peeled
  tomatoes

salt
freshly ground black pepper
2 tablespoons vinegar
2 level teaspoons sugar
2 tablespoons soy sauce

A good sauce to serve with grilled sausages or chops.

Measure the oil, onion and garlic into a bowl. Cook on **full power** for 5 minutes until the onion is soft. Add the tomatoes, salt and pepper, then cover and cook for a further 5 minutes on **full power** until the tomatoes are thick and pulpy. Stir in the vinegar, sugar and soy sauce: reheat on **full power** for 1 minute. Serve.

SPAGHETTI SAUCE

Power Level: Full   **Cooking Time:** 20 Minutes
Serves 4–6

2 tablespoons sunflower oil
1 large onion, chopped
2 sticks celery, sliced
1lb (450g) good quality lean
  minced beef
1oz (25g) flour
2 cloves garlic, crushed
2½oz (62g) can tomato purée

¼ pint (150ml) hot beef stock
¼ pint (150ml) red wine
14oz (397g) can peeled
  tomatoes
1 tablespoon redcurrant jelly
salt
freshly ground black pepper

One of the best recipes I know for Bolognaise Sauce, and the microwave cooks the mince to perfection. Serve with hot spaghetti and a sprinkling of Parmesan cheese.

Measure the oil into a microproof bowl with the onion, celery and beef. Stir well and cook on **full power** for 5 minutes. Stir in the flour, garlic and tomato purée, then gradually blend in the stock, wine, tomatoes, redcurrant jelly and seasoning. Cover with a lid or pierced clear film and cook on **full power** for 15 minutes, stirring twice during cooking, and again at the end of the cooking time. Ladle the sauce on top of hot spaghetti to serve.

HOLLANDAISE SAUCE

Power Levels: Full and Low   **Cooking Time:** 4 Minutes
Serves 3

4oz (100g) butter
juice of 1 lemon
2 egg yolks

salt
freshly ground black pepper

Serve hot with fish, vegetables or egg dishes. Essential to use a large bowl for cooking in so there is room enough to whisk the sauce thoroughly.

Measure the butter into a large bowl and heat on **full power** for 2 minutes until melted. Blend the lemon juice with the egg yolks and whisk into the hot butter. Cook on **low power** for 2 minutes, watching the sauce like a hawk to ensure it doesn't boil. Season to taste, whisk well and serve straightaway.

Pot pourri
Rose petals for pot pourri can be dried in the microwave in the same way as herbs. Sandwich them in one layer between two pieces of kitchen paper and heat on **full power** for about **2 minutes** until dry. The colour is kept bright – especially the reds.

CUSTARD

Power Level: Full   **Cooking Time:** 3 Minutes
Serves 3–4

1–2 tablespoons sugar
1 tablespoon custard powder
½ pint (300ml) milk

So much simpler than making custard in a saucepan – and easier to wash up, too!

Measure the sugar and custard powder into a large microproof jug with a little of the milk and blend until smooth. Gradually blend in the remaining milk. Cook on **full power** for 3 minutes, whisking twice during cooking. Whisk again thoroughly at the end of cooking until the custard is thick and smooth.

REAL CHOCOLATE SAUCE

Power Levels: Full and Medium
Cooking Time: 6½ Minutes   **Makes** about ½ pint (300ml)

1oz (25g) hard margarine
2 rounded dessertspoons
  cocoa powder, sieved

5oz (150g) caster sugar
4 fl oz (120ml) water
3 drops vanilla essence

Quick and easy to prepare, and a good standby to serve with ice cream and profiteroles.

Measure the margarine into a microproof bowl and heat on **full power** for 1 minute. Stir in the cocoa and sugar. Bring the water to the boil in a microproof jug on **full power** for 1½ minutes, then stir into the cocoa mixture. Return to the cooker and heat on **medium power** for 4 minutes. Whisk in the vanilla essence and serve either hot or cold.

Hot and Cold Puddings

Puddings are one area in which your family will feel the microwave has been a great investment! A pudding can be produced so quickly and with such little fuss that it becomes more and more difficult for me to get out of serving one at the end of a meal!

Favourites such as rice pudding, suet pudding and upside-down puddings can all be made in a matter of minutes instead of the longer cooking time I usually have to allow. Fruit cooks beautifully, too, and retains all its flavour and colour. Cooked fruit can easily be transformed into a more substantial pudding (a crumble or pie, or a Summer Pudding (page 125), or is equally delicious served on its own with custard or a little whipped cream.

No lengthy pre-soaking is necessary when cooking dried fruits or compotes, and again, the cooking time is greatly reduced. And you can serve a fruit compote chilled for breakfast the following day – if there happens to be any left over from supper.

I still prefer to cook my Christmas puddings in the traditional way, as I have yet to find a microwave recipe which I like as much as my usual one. However, you can reheat your pudding – like other suet or sponge puds – on **full power** for 2–3 minutes, then serve it with your favourite sauce.

STEWED FRUIT

Fruit cooks beautifully in the microwave and retains its shape well. Do remember that it will continue to cook for a few minutes from residual heat when it comes out of the microwave, so don't be tempted to overcook the fruits if they appear not to be quite done when they first come out of the microwave.

APPLE
Peel, core and slice 1lb (450g) cooking apples, arrange them in a bowl and sprinkle with 2–4oz (50–100g) sugar to taste. Cover with pierced clear film and cook on **full power** for 6–8 minutes, stirring once during cooking.

GOOSEBERRIES
Top and tail 1lb (450g) gooseberries, put into a bowl and sprinkle with 4–6oz (100–175g) sugar to taste. Cover with pierced clear film and cook on **full power** for 4 minutes, stirring once during cooking.

PLUMS
Wash and stone 1lb (450g) plums, arrange them in a bowl and sprinkle with 2–4oz (50–100g) sugar to taste. Cover with pierced clear film, then cook on **full power** for 5–7 minutes, stirring once during cooking.

SOFT FRUITS
Top and tail or hull 1lb (450g) soft fruits. Put them in a bowl,

sprinkle with 3–4oz (75–100g) sugar to taste and cover with pierced clear film. Cook on **full power** for 3–5 minutes, stirring once during cooking.

RHUBARB AND ORANGE

Wipe, then trim and slice 1½lb (675g) rhubarb into a bowl, add the grated rind and the juice of a large orange and sprinkle with 6oz (175g) sugar. Mix together lightly and cover with pierced clear film. Cook on **full power** for 5 minutes, stirring once during cooking. Leave to stand for a few minutes before serving warm with custard, or chill well and serve with a blob of whipped cream.

PLUMS AND ALMONDS

Power Level: Full   **Cooking Time:** 5 Minutes
Serves 3

1lb (450g) plums or damsons   2oz (50g) toasted flaked
3oz (75g) sugar, to taste   almonds
                                                         cream for serving

Serve either warm or well chilled. Personally, I prefer them really well chilled – with cream.

Wash and stone the plums or damsons and put them into a bowl with the sugar. Cover with pierced clear film and cook on **full power** for 5 minutes. Stir once during cooking. Allow to cool, then chill in the refrigerator for several hours. Sprinkle with almonds and serve with cream.

CHILLED BLACKCURRANT CREAMS

Power Level: Full   **Cooking Time:** 4–5 Minutes
Serves 4

8oz (225g) blackcurrants
4oz (100g) light muscovado
   sugar, or to taste
2 tablespoons boiling water

¼ pint (142ml) carton double
   cream
¼ pint (142ml) carton Greek-
   style natural yoghurt

*A quick dessert; you can use frozen fruit – just cook it from frozen on **full power**, draining off any excess juices as it cooks.*

Put the fruit into a microproof bowl with 2 tablespoons of the sugar and the water. Cook on **full power** until blackcurrants are soft – this takes 4–5 minutes. Taste for sweetness and allow to cool. Divide the fruit between 4 tall glasses. Whip the cream until it just holds its shape, then fold in the yoghurt. Spoon over the blackcurrants and top with the remaining sugar.

Chill in the refrigerator for about 10 minutes, to allow the sugar to dissolve a little into the creamy topping. Serve with crisp biscuits.

SOFT FRUIT FLAN

Power Level: Full   **Cooking Time:** About 5 Minutes
Serves 6

6oz (175g) plain flour
3oz (75g) butter
about 1½ tablespoons cold
    water

3 tablespoons apricot jam or
    redcurrant jelly
1 tablespoon water
whipped cream for serving

For the filling
12oz–1lb (350–450g) soft
    fruit in season, or poached
    fruit

*Bake a buttery flan case and fill it with soft fruits in season, or
sliced poached plums, apricots or peaches. Melt a little jam to
make a delicious glaze.*

Measure the flour into a bowl and rub in the butter until the
mixture resembles fine breadcrumbs. Add sufficient water to
mix to a firm dough. Roll out the pastry on a lightly floured
surface and use to line an 8in (10cm) ceramic flan dish. Prick
the base well with a fork and chill in the refrigerator for about
10 minutes. Line the flan with a piece of kitchen paper and
cook in the microwave on **full power** for about 4 minutes.

Whilst the flan case is still hot, brush evenly with a little
melted jam to seal the pastry. Leave to cool, then fill the cooled
case with soft fruit (strawberries, blackberries and redcurrants) arranged in circles, or sliced poached fruit.

Melt the jam or jelly with the water in a small bowl on **full
power** for 1 minute, stirring once, then brush over the fruit to
glaze. Serve with whipped cream.

SUMMER PUDDING

Power Level: Full   **Cooking Time:** 8 Minutes
Serves 6

6–8 large slices white bread   6 tablespoons water
12oz (350g) rhubarb   8oz (225g) strawberries
8oz (225g) blackcurrants   8oz (225g) raspberries
8oz (225g) granulated sugar

The same fruit filling can be served just with fresh cream as a rich, red fruit salad. If the suggested fruits are not available, use loganberries and redcurrants with a mixture of either fresh or frozen fruit.

Cut the crusts from the bread and put aside one slice for the top. Use the remainder of the bread to line the base and sides of a 2 pint (1.2 litre) round, fairly shallow microproof dish.

Cut the rhubarb into ½ inch (1.25cm) pieces and put in a bowl with the blackcurrants. Add the sugar and water; cover with pierced clear film and cook on **full power** for 7 minutes, stirring once during cooking. Add the strawberries and raspberries and cook for a further 1 minute.

Turn the mixture into the prepared dish, reserving a little of the juice. Place the reserved slice of bread on top, and bend the other slices of bread lining the sides towards the centre. Put a saucer on top, pressing down a little until the juice rises to the top of the dish. Spoon any remaining juice down the sides of the dish so that every slice is well soaked. Chill overnight in the refrigerator.

Turn out just before serving and serve with lashings of cream.

BAKED APPLES

Power Level: Full   **Cooking Time:** 5½–6 Minutes
Serves 4

4 medium cooking apples
3oz (75g) soft brown sugar
2oz (50g) sultanas

2oz (50g) chopped walnuts
2 tablespoons water
2oz (50g) butter

Cooked in the microwave in a mere fraction of the time they would normally take in a conventional oven. Serve warm with lashings of custard.

Core the apples, score the skin all round each apple to prevent them from bursting during cooking. Stand in a microproof dish as far apart as possible. Mix the sugar, sultanas and nuts together in a bowl and press the mixture into the centre of the apples. Pour the water into the dish. Dot each apple with a little butter and cook on **full power** for 5½–6 minutes.

Allow to stand for about 5 minutes, then serve with the cooking juices poured over the fruit.

MIDSUMMER FRUITS

Power Level: Full   **Cooking Time:** 6 Minutes
Serves 6

1 large orange
4 cloves
1lb (450g) blackcurrants
8oz (225g) blackberries
6oz (175g) sugar

¼ pint (150ml) water
8oz (225g) raspberries
1lb (450g) pears, peeled,
  cored and sliced

This is especially good served with lightly whipped cream or ice cream.

Cut strips of peel from the orange, stick with the cloves and place in a microproof bowl with the blackcurrants, blackberries, sugar and water. Cover with pierced clear film and cook on **full power** for 6 minutes, stirring once during cooking. Leave to cool, then chill thoroughly.

Remove and discard the orange rind. Cut the orange into segments. Stir in the raspberries, pears and orange segments just before serving.

SPICED FRUIT COMPOTE

Power Level: Full   **Cooking Time:** 18–20 Minutes
Serves 6–8

2oz (50g) dried figs
2oz (50g) dried apricots
2oz (50g) dried peaches
2oz (50g) dried prunes
2oz (50g) dried apple rings
2oz (50g) sultanas

¾ pint (750ml) water
4oz (100g) light muscovado
    sugar
1 strip lemon rind
1 teaspoon ground nutmeg
1 teaspoon ground cinnamon

Delicious served really well chilled with natural yoghurt.

Measure all the ingredients into a large microproof bowl; mix well. Cover with pierced clear film and cook on **full power** for 18–20 minutes, stirring and pushing the fruit down into the liquid twice during cooking. Allow to stand until cold, then remove and discard the strip of lemon rind. Chill in the refrigerator, preferably overnight.

SUET PUDDING

Power Level: Full   **Cooking Time:** 6–8 Minutes
Serves 4–6

2 tablespoons raspberry jam
5oz (150g) self raising flour
¼ teaspoon salt
2oz (50g) shredded suet

2oz (50g) caster sugar
1 egg, beaten
¼ pint (150ml) milk

A satisfying and warming winter pudding. The microwave makes suet-based puddings easy, by cutting out the laborious hours of steaming in a hot, damp kitchen.

Lightly grease a 2 pint (1.2 litre) pudding basin, and spoon the jam into the base of the basin.

Measure the dry ingredients into a large bowl, make a well in the centre and add the egg and milk. Mix to a smooth soft consistency, then spoon over the jam. Level out top and cook on **full power** for 6–8 minutes. Leave to stand for about 5 minutes, then carefully turn out the pudding on to a serving plate and serve warm.

Softening honey
Soften those last few tablespoons of honey, golden syrup or liquid glucose left in the jar. Allow up to 1 minute on **full power**. Particularly good if it has slightly crystallized, and it's so much easier to scoop out.

APRICOT SPONGE PUDDING

Power Level: Full   **Cooking Time:** 7 Minutes
Serves 4

15oz (425g) can apricot
  halves, drained and juice
  reserved
2oz (50g) butter
2oz (50g) caster sugar
2oz (50g) self raising flour
2oz (50g) ground almonds

1 egg, beaten
1oz (25g) toasted flaked
  almonds

For the sauce
8oz (225g) apricot jam

*All baked in 10 minutes from storecupboard ingredients! A
little sieved icing sugar makes the top look extra smart.*

Arrange the apricot halves in the bottom of a 2 pint (1.2 litre)
deep ceramic dish or Pyrex soufflé dish. Measure the butter,
sugar, flour, ground almonds and egg into a bowl and beat
well until thoroughly blended. Spoon over the apricots, level
out top, sprinkle with almonds and cook on **full power** for 5
minutes. Allow to stand for 3 minutes.

Whilst the pudding is standing, prepare the sauce. Mix the
jam with the juice reserved from the apricots in a microproof
bowl. Cook on **full power** for 2 minutes; mix well and serve
with the pudding.

PINEAPPLE UPSIDE-DOWN PUDDING

Power Level: Full   **Cooking Time:** 5 Minutes
Serves 4

For the sponge
3oz (75g) self raising flour
3oz (75g) soft margarine
3oz (75g) caster sugar
1 egg, beaten
3 tablespoons pineapple juice
½ level teaspoon baking
  powder

For the topping
2oz (50g) light brown sugar
8oz (227g) can pineapple
  rings, drained and juice
  reserved
2 glacé cherries, halved

*A real family favourite: it never fails and always looks good.
Serve with custard or ice cream.*

Lightly butter a 7-inch (17.5cm) round cake container and
sprinkle with the soft brown sugar for the topping. Set aside.
Place all the ingredients for the sponge in a bowl and lightly
mix together until thoroughly blended.

Arrange 4 pineapple rings in the base of the cake container
and put a halved cherry in the centre of each ring, cut side
uppermost. Spread the sponge mixture over the pineapple and
level out top. Cook on **full power** for 5 minutes. Leave to
stand in the dish for about 5 minutes, then turn out, pineapple
uppermost, and serve warm.

INDIVIDUAL TREACLE PUDDINGS

Power Levels: Full and Medium
Cooking Time: 3–4 Minutes   **Serves** 6

4oz (100g) soft margarine	4oz (100g) self raising flour
4oz (100g) caster sugar	3 tablespoons milk
2 eggs, beaten	3 tablespoons golden syrup

So much easier than steaming puddings – and the cooking time is cut dramatically. Serve these individual puddings with thick custard or vanilla ice cream.

Lightly grease 6 cups, microproof ramekin dishes or dariole containers.

Measure all the ingredients, except the syrup, into a bowl and mix lightly until thoroughly blended. Heat the syrup for a few seconds on **medium power** to make it easier to manage and divide between the prepared dishes. Divide the sponge mixture between the dishes, carefully spooning it on top of the syrup. Level the tops.

Arrange in the microwave in a circle and cook on **full power** for 3–4 minutes. The top of the sponges may look a little damp and sticky, but leave to stand for 3 minutes and they should dry from the residual heat.

Carefully turn out the puddings into serving dishes and serve warm.

RICE PUDDING

Power Level: Low   **Cooking Time:** 35–40 Minutes
Serves 4

2oz (50g) pudding rice
1 pint (600ml) milk
1oz (25g) sugar

1oz (25g) butter
a little grated nutmeg

I always used to cook this in a low oven for up to 2 hours, so it is a real boon to be able to have such a rich, creamy result in such a little time now.

Measure all the ingredients except the nutmeg into a large bowl. Cover with pierced clear film and cook on **low power** for 35–40 minutes, stirring every 10 minutes until thick and creamy. Sprinkle with a little grated nutmeg to serve.

LEMON SEMOLINA PUDDING

Power Level: Full   **Cooking Time:** 7 Minutes
Serves 4

2oz (50g) semolina
1½oz (40g) caster sugar
grated rind of 1 lemon

1 pint (600ml) milk
½oz (15g) butter

A good way of using up any extra milk which you might happen to have in the fridge.

Measure the semolina into a microproof bowl with the sugar, lemon rind and milk. Mix well and cook on **full power** for 7 minutes, stirring well twice during cooking. Add butter and mix well until smooth. Serve straightaway.

CRÈME CARAMEL

Power Levels: Full and Medium
Cooking Time: 16–17 Minutes   **Serves** 4

4oz (100g) granulated or caster sugar	2 eggs
4 tablespoons water	1oz (25g) vanilla sugar
	½ pint (300ml) milk

Do take care with the caramel when it comes out of the cooker as it will be exceedingly hot. If making one large Crème Caramel, make the caramel in the dish you are going to cook it in, a toughened glass Pyrex type, or an ovenproof soufflé dish. If you have no vanilla sugar, add 1 teaspoon vanilla essence to the custard.

Measure the sugar and water into a large Pyrex bowl. Cook on **full power** for 2 minutes, then stir to ensure all the sugar is dissolved. Return caramel to the cooker and cook on **full power** for 10 minutes. Keep an eye on the caramel, it should turn a rich, golden toffee colour. If it has not reached this colour, cook for a further 30 seconds or so, taking care it does not burn. Divide the caramel between four ramekin dishes or containers straightaway.

Beat the eggs in a bowl with the vanilla sugar till blended. Warm the milk on **medium power** for 1½ minutes, then stir it into the beaten eggs. Strain through a sieve and divide between the four ramekins. Stand the ramekin dishes in the microwave and cook on **medium power** for 2½–3 minutes, or until the custard has set. Remove, allow to cool, then chill in the refrigerator until required.

CARAMEL ORANGES

The caramel could also be used for Caramel Oranges. Cut all the peel and pith from the oranges with a sharp knife. Slice the fruit then reassemble into rounds and arrange in a serving dish. Pour over the cooled caramel and decorate with thin strips of orange zest which have been cooked in water on **full power** for about 3 minutes until tender.

BLACKBERRY MOUSSE

Power Level: Full   **Cooking Time:** 6 Minutes
Serves 6

1lb (450g) blackberries
4oz (100g) caster sugar
juice of ½ lemon
½oz (15g) powdered gelatine

3 tablespoons cold water
2 egg whites
¼ pint (150ml) whipping cream, whipped

Do be sure that the blackberry purée is really beginning to set before folding in the cream and egg whites, otherwise they will separate out like a honeycomb mousse!

Reserve 6 blackberries and measure the rest with the caster sugar and lemon juice into a microproof bowl, cover with clear film and cook on **full power** for 5 minutes. Measure the gelatine and cold water into a small bowl and leave to stand for 3 minutes to form a sponge.

Sieve the blackberry mixture to remove all the seeds. Stir the soaked gelatine into the purée and cook on **full power** for 1 minute to dissolve the gelatine. Remove from the microwave and leave to cool until thick and pulpy. Whisk the egg whites until they form soft peaks, then fold into the setting blackberry purée with the whipped cream, until thoroughly blended.

Divide the mousse between 6 individual glasses – I prefer tall stemmed ones – and chill in the refrigerator until set. Decorate with the reserved blackberries. If liked, serve with a swirl of cream piped on top.

Tea-Time Bakes

I must be honest and admit that I only use my microwave for making cakes when I'm really in a hurry and need one to bake and serve on the same day. I'm sure there are many people who will not agree, but it isn't easy to achieve the texture we like, and there's no crusty topping to a sponge. However, the children love making cup cakes to ice and eat straightaway, and my caramel shortbread never lasts long!

On the whole, I feel the microwave comes into its own when helping to prepare the ingredients for baking: melting chocolate so well and quickly, without it having to be done over a pan of water; softening almond paste to cover a cake in about a minute (on **medium power**); softening sugar that has grown rock-hard in the jar, and melting apricot jam to make a quick glaze.

My tips? I find it best not to over-beat or over-process a mixture before baking, but just to blend all the ingredients gently until smooth. A tablespoon of golden syrup stirred into the mixture – or substituting 2oz (50g) ground almonds for the equivalent amount of flour – greatly improves its keeping quality.

Bread, on the other hand, works well, though I always top a loaf with sesame seeds or poppy seeds to improve its pale, unbaked look! I have found most success with using ordinary dried yeast in my recipes: the easy-blend types which you add directly to the flour don't give the best results in *my* microwave. Here are my best bakes . . .

VICTORIA SANDWICH

Power Level: Full   **Cooking Time:** 5 Minutes
Serves 6–8

4oz (100g) caster sugar
4oz (100g) soft margarine
2 eggs, beaten
4oz (100g) self raising flour

2 tablespoons milk
1 level tablespoon golden
 syrup

When made in the microwave, the colour is pale and the top of the cake is often tacky, so it should be iced for best results. Wrap it in clear film as soon as it comes out of the cooker to help prevent it drying out. (I find that it rises better if made in one container.) Split and fill it later.

Measure the caster sugar and margarine into a mixing bowl, cream together until light and fluffy, then gradually add the beaten eggs, mixing well after each addition. Put in 1 tablespoon of flour with the last amount of egg as this prevents the mixture curdling.

Fold in the rest of the flour and then mix in the milk. Finally, stir in the golden syrup. Turn the mixture into a 7 inch (18cm) soufflé dish and cook on **full power** for 5 minutes. Leave it to stand for an extra 5 minutes after cooking, then turn it out on to a cooling rack and wrap in clear film. Split the cake in half horizontally, and decorate when the cake is cool.

To Decorate

1   Spread 1 tablespoon of jam over the surface of the middle
of the cake. Cover this with butter cream using 2oz (50g) soft
butter and 5oz (150g) sieved icing sugar beaten together until
smooth. Sandwich the cake together and sprinkle a little extra
sieved icing sugar on top.

2   Sandwich the two halves together with 2 tablespoons jam.
Make some glacé icing by measuring 6oz (175g) icing sugar
into a bowl and mix with about 1 tablespoon water. Leave 2
tablespoons icing in the bowl and spread the rest over the top
of the cake. Add a drop of food colouring to the remaining icing
and put this into a small polythene bag. Snip a small hole in
the corner of the bag and trickle the icing in lines over the top
of the cake. Feather this with a skewer.

3   Spread 1 tablespoon strawberry jam over the surface of the
middle of the cake and top this with ¼ pint (150ml) whipped
cream. Place a few strawberries on the cream and sandwich
the two halves of the cake together. Sprinkle sieved icing
sugar on top. Serve this on special occasions.

ALMOND FLAPJACKS

Power Level: Full   **Cooking Time:** 4 Minutes
Makes 9

4oz (100g) demerara sugar   4oz (100g) soft margarine
5oz (150g) rolled oats   1 level tablespoon golden
2oz (50g) chopped almonds   syrup

Although these look pale, they are lovely and crisp in texture.

Lightly grease a 7 inch (17.5cm.) square, shallow microproof
dish. Measure the sugar, oats and almonds into a bowl, mix
together, then work in the margarine and golden syrup. Press
the mixture into the greased dish, levelling the top with a

metal spoon, then cook on **full power** for 4 minutes. When cooked, divide into 9 squares while still hot.

Allow to get cold before lifting the squares out. Store in an airtight tin.

CHOCOLATE CAKE

Power Level: Full   **Cooking Time:** 13½ Minutes

6½oz (190g) plain flour
2 level tablespoons cocoa
  powder
1 level teaspoon bicarbonate
  of soda
1 level teaspoon baking
  powder
5oz (150g) caster sugar
2 tablespoons golden syrup
2 eggs, beaten

¼ pint (150ml) sunflower oil
¼ pint (150ml) milk

For the icing
2oz (50g) butter
4 level tablespoons cocoa,
  sieved
2 tablespoons milk
5oz (150g) icing sugar, sieved

This cake works really well in the microwave and will keep reasonably moist for about 3 days after baking if kept in an airtight tin.

Line the bases of two 8 inch (20cm) microproof sandwich cake containers with a circle of kitchen paper.

Measure the dry ingredients into a large bowl and make a well in the centre. Add syrup, eggs, oil and milk and beat well until evenly blended. Divide between the two containers.

Bake each cake separately in the microwave for about 5 minutes each on **full power** until well risen. Remove from the microwave, allow to stand for about 3 minutes, then turn out, peel off the paper, wrap in clear film and finish cooling on a wire rack.

For the icing, measure the butter into a microproof bowl and heat on **full power** for 2 minutes, or until melted. Stir in the cocoa and cook for a further 1½ minutes. Remove from the microwave and stir in the milk and icing sugar. Beat well until smooth, then leave on one side until beginning to thicken. Sandwich the cakes together with half the icing and spread the remainder on top, swirling with a knife to give an attractive appearance.

CHOCOLATE AND NUT CUP CAKES

Power Level: Full   **Cooking Time:** 6 Minutes
Makes about 12

For the cakes
3½oz (90g) self raising flour
½oz (15g) cocoa, sieved
2oz (50g) soft margarine
2oz (50g) soft brown sugar
1oz (25g) chopped walnuts
1 egg
3 tablespoons milk

For the topping
1½oz (40g) butter
1oz (25g) cocoa, sieved
4oz (100g) icing sugar, sieved
1 tablespoon milk

These are ideal for a children's tea party. They are best eaten on the day they are made.

Measure all the ingredients for the cakes into a bowl and gently stir together until thoroughly blended. Line a microproof muffin dish with paper cases, or use double thickness paper cases and spoon a teaspoon of the mixture into each. Arrange in a circle on 1 large microproof plate. Cook on **full power** for 2 minutes. Lift out of the muffin dish, or off the plate, and allow to cool on a wire rack. Repeat with the remaining mixture.

For the icing, measure the butter into a bowl and heat on **full power** for 1 minute. Stir in the cocoa and cook for a further 1 minute, then remove from the microwave and stir in the icing sugar and milk. Beat until smooth. Allow to cool and, when just beginning to set, spoon a little over each cup cake and level out evenly. Allow to set completely before serving.

STICKY GINGERBREAD

Power Level: Medium   **Cooking Time:** 16 Minutes
Makes 12 squares

4oz (100g) hard margarine
4oz (100g) dark muscovado
  sugar
4oz (100g) black treacle
2 eggs, beaten

6oz (175g) plain flour
2 teaspoons ground ginger
1 teaspoon cinnamon
¼ pint (150ml) milk

Leave this to cool completely in the cooking dish before turning out.

Lightly grease and line the base of a rectangular microproof dish, 5 × 9 inches (13 × 22.5cm), with a piece of kitchen paper.

Measure the margarine, sugar and black treacle into a microproof bowl and heat on **medium power** for 3 minutes, then stir well until the margarine has melted and the mixture is thoroughly blended. Stir in the eggs, flour, ginger and cinnamon and mix well. Heat milk on **medium power** for 2 minutes until hand-hot and stir into the ginger mixture. Beat well until smooth.

Pour into the prepared dish and cook on **medium power** for 11 minutes. The top of the gingerbread will still be sticky but a skewer should come out clean when pushed into the centre of the cake. Allow to cool completely, turn out and divide into 12 squares.

LITTLE HONEY BUNS

Power Levels: Full and Low
Cooking Time: about 15 Minutes   **Makes** 32

3½oz (100g) Cadbury's
  Bournville chocolate
4oz (100g) soft margarine
3oz (75g) caster sugar
2 eggs
5oz (150g) self raising flour,
  sieved

For the topping
8oz (225g) cream cheese
2oz (50g) caster sugar
1 egg
¼ teaspoon baking powder
1 teaspoon ground cinnamon
2 tablespoons runny honey

These make good coffee-time treats. Cook in batches of ten or so, and if you don't have a suitable microproof bun pan, use double paper cake cases.

Break the chocolate into a microproof bowl and melt on **low power** for 4 minutes. Cream the margarine and sugar together, then beat in the eggs, one at a time, beating well between each addition. Add the melted chocolate, then fold in the sieved flour. Divide the mixture between 32 paper cake cases; set aside.

For the topping, mix together the cheese and sugar until soft, then beat in the egg and baking powder. Drop a good teaspoonful of cheese mixture on to each bun and dust with cinnamon. Place paper cases into a microproof bun tray, or arrange them round the edge of a turntable (or in a ring on the floor of the cooker cavity) and cook on **full power** for 2½–3 minutes.

Leave to stand for 5 minutes, then remove the buns from the tray. Repeat in batches until all the little buns are cooked. Brush each with a little warmed honey before serving.

BUTTERSCOTCH FUDGE CAKE

Power Levels: Full and Low   **Cooking Time:** 24 Minutes
Serves 8–10

4oz (100g) Cadbury's
  Bourneville chocolate
2 fl oz (60ml) sunflower oil
6 fl oz (180ml) water
4oz (100g) margarine
8oz (225g) caster sugar
10oz (300g) self raising flour
2 eggs
4 fl oz (120ml) milk
½ teaspoon bicarbonate of
  soda

For the frosting
4oz (100g) butter
4oz (100g) soft brown sugar
3 tablespoons milk
1 teaspoon vanilla essence
12oz (350g) icing sugar,
  sieved
cocoa powder for sprinkling

Quick to make and keeps well in an airtight tin. The frosting keeps it moist.

Break the chocolate into a bowl, add the oil, water and margarine and heat on **full power** for 4 minutes, stirring after every minute. Beat in the remaining cake ingredients until the mixture is smooth. Turn it into an 8 inch (20cm) base-lined soufflé dish and cook on **low power** for about 20 minutes, until the cake is cooked and well risen.

Leave to stand in the dish for 10 minutes, before turning out on to a wire rack to cool completely.

For the frosting, put the butter into a microproof bowl with the sugar and cook on **full power** for 3 minutes, stirring well after every minute. Stir in the milk and vanilla essence, then microwave on **full power** for 1 minute. Beat in the icing sugar and continue beating hard until cooled and thickened.

Split the cooled cake in half and sandwich the halves together with a layer of frosting, then cover the cake completely with the remaining frosting, swirling it with the blade of a knife. Dust the top lightly with cocoa powder when set.

CHOCOLATE CARAMEL SHORTBREAD

Power Levels: Full and Medium
Cooking Time: about 18 Minutes   **Makes** 16

For the base
4oz (100g) soft margarine
2oz (50g) caster sugar
6oz (150g) plain flour

For the caramel
4oz (100g) margarine
3oz (75g) caster sugar
2 level tablespoons golden
  syrup
6oz (193g) can condensed
  milk

For the topping
3½oz (100g) bar plain
  chocolate

Using the microwave for this makes it safer than heating the caramel in a heavy saucepan.

Measure all the ingredients for the base into a bowl and work to a firm dough.

Press the dough into a rectangular microproof dish measuring 5 × 9 inches (13 × 22.5cm) with the back of a metal spoon, or the palm of the hand. Prick with a fork and cook on **full power** for 1 minute, then on **medium power** for a further 4½ minutes. Leave to stand until cold.

For the caramel, measure all the ingredients into a deep microproof bowl. Cook on **medium power** for 6 minutes, stir well, then continue to cook on **medium power** for a further 4–5 minutes until caramel coloured. Beat well until smooth and spread over the shortbread base. *Do take great care* as the mixture will be extremely hot. Leave to set.

Break the chocolate into a microproof bowl and heat on **medium power** for about 1½ minutes. Stir until smooth, return to the cooker if necessary to ensure all the chocolate has melted. Spread evenly over the caramel topping, and lightly swirl the top with a fork. Leave for several hours to set before dividing into fingers. Store in an airtight tin.

MINCE PIES

Power Levels: Full and Medium
Cooking time: 5 Minutes per batch   **Makes** 16

For the pastry
8oz (225g) plain flour
2oz (50g) lard
2oz (50g) margarine
about 8 teaspoons water

For the filling
about 8oz (225g) mincemeat
a little icing sugar, to dust

Do not expect the pastry to brown during cooking; the pies may look rather pale when they first come out of the oven but once assembled and dusted with a little icing sugar they are perfectly acceptable.

Measure the flour into a bowl and rub in the fats until the mixture resembles fine breadcrumbs. Add just enough water to bind to a dough, then knead until smooth. Roll out on a lightly floured surface. Cut out 16 circles with a 4 inch (10cm) fluted pastry cutter and use to line a microwave muffin pan. It will be necessary to bake the pastry in 2–3 batches depending on the size of the pan.

Prick the base of each pastry case with a fork. Cook on **full power** for 2½ minutes. If the middles have risen during cooking, carefully press them down as soon as they come out of the cooker. Lift out of the pan with a rounded knife and cool on a wire rack. Cook the remaining pastry cases.

For the tops, cut out 16 small rounds from the remaining pastry with a 3 inch (7.5cm) fluted cutter. Arrange in a circle on a piece of greaseproof paper and cook for 1½ minutes.

To fill the pies, warm the mincemeat on **medium power** for 1 minute, stir, then divide between the pastry cases. Top each with one of the circles of pastry and dust with icing sugar to serve.

SCONES

Power Level: Medium   **Cooking Time:** 4 Minutes
Makes about 8

4oz (100g) self raising flour
1oz (25g) margarine
½oz (15g) caster sugar

1oz (25g) dried mixed fruit
generous ⅛ pint (65ml) milk
a little beaten egg to glaze

These must *be eaten straight from the oven whilst they are warm and soft.*

Measure the flour into a bowl and rub in the margarine. Stir in the sugar, fruit and milk and mix to a soft dough. Turn out on to a lightly floured surface and knead lightly. Roll out to ¼ inch (5mm) thickness and cut into rounds with a 2 inch (5cm) fluted cutter.

Arrange the scones in a circle on a sheet of greaseproof paper, glaze with a little beaten egg and cook on **medium power** for 4 minutes. Allow to cool slightly and serve warm with butter and jam.

CHEESE SCONES
Make as above, but substitute 2oz (50g) grated Cheddar cheese and a little seasoning instead of the fruit and sugar. Serve warm with butter.

BREAD

Power Level: Full **Cooking Time:** 5 Minutes
Makes a 1lb (450g) loaf

½ pint (300ml) water
2 teaspoons dried yeast
2 teaspoons sugar
8oz (225g) wholewheat flour
8oz (225g) strong plain white
  flour

2 teaspoons salt
1oz (25g) lard
a little beaten egg, to glaze
sesame or poppy seeds

Bread from the microwave is surprisingly delicious to eat, but it does look rather pale and 'uncooked'; I always glaze the loaf and sprinkle a few poppy seeds or sesame seeds on top before cooking to improve its appearance. Eat on the day of making.

Measure the water into a jug and heat on **full power** for about 1 minute until warm. Stir in the yeast and the sugar and leave in a warm place until beginning to froth.

Measure the flours, salt and fat into a large bowl and rub in the fat. Add the yeast liquid to the flour and mix to an elastic dough. Turn out on to a floured surface and knead for about 5 minutes. (This can be done in a processor and will need 1 minute of processing.) Place in a bowl, cover with greased clear film and leave in a warm place until the dough has doubled in size.

Turn out of the bowl, 'knock back' the dough, shape into a 'loaf' and lift into a lightly oiled 1lb (450g) microproof loaf container. Cover with the clear film and leave in a warm place until the dough has risen to the top of the container. Glaze with a little beaten egg and sprinkle with a few seeds. Cook on **full power** for 4 minutes. Leave to stand for 1 minute, then turn out of the container and allow to cool on a rack.

Pickles and Preserves

Making jams and pickles in the microwave really does take all the hard work out of preserving. The results are excellent. The preserves have a fresh, true flavour and a rich, bright, natural colour, and they need very little attention during cooking. However, the microwave can only cope with making a small quantity at a time, so I'd advise you to stick to your traditional method and use a large preserving pan when you need to take advantage of a glut of fruit, tomatoes, or make a stock of marmalade when Seville oranges are in season.

But there are other benefits: the microwave relieves you of a damp, steamy kitchen, and most of the pickling smells are confined inside the cooker. This is also a fairly safe method of preserving, with less likelihood of burnt fingers – though you *must* still wear oven gloves as the containers get very hot indeed, especially with sugar mixtures.

The basic principles of preserving remain the same; it is essential to use a large bowl or container for cooking, since the preserves will boil up fiercely. Watch for this. The setting point can be tested in the usual way, by spooning a little on to a chilled saucer, allowing it to cool, then pushing it with a fingertip. If the surface wrinkles, the setting point has been reached.

Jam jars may also be sterilized in the microwave. Half-fill each jar with cold water, heat on **full power** for 2–3 minutes until boiling, then carefully remove the hot jars from the microwave, swirl the water round the jar, then pour it away. Drain the jars upside down on clean kitchen paper, then fill, seal and label them in the usual way.

SPICED VINEGAR

Power Level: Full   **Cooking Time:** 4 Minutes
For 2 pints (1.2 litres) vinegar

2 pints (1.2 litres) vinegar
6 whole cloves
1 stick cinnamon

1 inch (2.5cm) piece peeled
  root ginger
8 peppercorns

Spicing vinegar improves the flavour of pickles enormously and is well worth it!

Measure the vinegar into a large microproof bowl with the cloves, cinnamon, ginger and peppercorns. Cover with pierced clear film and heat on **full power** for 4 minutes. Allow to get cold, then strain the vinegar and discard the spices. If the vinegar is not going to be used straightaway, return to the bottle and seal. Use for pickled onions, cooking red cabbage etc.

TOMATO CHUTNEY

Power Level: Full   **Cooking Time:** 15–20 Minutes
Makes about 2½lb (1.25kg)

1½lb (675g) green or red
    tomatoes, skinned and
    sliced
1 small red pepper, cored,
    seeded and chopped
1 large onion, chopped
6oz (175g) Bramley apples,
    weighed when peeled,
    cored and chopped

3oz (75g) raisins
1 level tablespoon salt
½ inch (1cm) piece peeled
    root ginger
a little Cayenne pepper
6oz (175g) dark or light
    muscovado sugar
½ pint (300ml) malt vinegar

Homemade chutney is a splendid addition to any storecup-
board. Make this with the last of the home-grown tomatoes, or
when there's a glut.

Measure all the ingredients into a large microproof bowl and
mix well. Cook on **full power** for 15–20 minutes until the
mixture is thick and pulpy, stirring twice during cooking.
Remove the piece of root ginger and pot in clean warm jars.
Seal with plastic or vinegar-proof lids.

RHUBARB AND RAISIN CHUTNEY

Power Level: Full **Cooking Time:** 15–20 Minutes
Makes about 2½lb (1.25kg)

1lb (450g) rhubarb, trimmed
and thinly sliced
8oz (225g) raisins
8oz (225g) light or dark
muscovado sugar
½ pint (300ml) cider vinegar
¼ pint (150ml) water

½ teaspoon allspice
2–3 whole cloves
½ teaspoon salt
1 teaspoon mustard seeds
¼ teaspoon celery seeds
2 onions, finely chopped

*Here's another good chutney for using your garden store of
rhubarb.*

Measure all the ingredients into a large microproof bowl and
mix well. Cook on **full power** for 15–20 minutes, until the
mixture is thick and pulpy, stirring twice during cooking. Pot
in clean, warm jars, allow to cool and seal with plastic or
vinegar-proof lids.

APPLE AND MOLASSES CHUTNEY

Power Level: Full **Cooking Time:** 25 Minutes
Makes about 2lb (900g)

1lb (450g) Bramley apples,
peeled, cored and sliced
1 large onion, chopped
1 tablespoon salt
good ½ pint (300ml) pickling
vinegar
8oz (225g) dark muscovado
sugar or molasses sugar

2 fat cloves garlic, crushed
6oz (175g) sultanas
2 level tablespoons dry
mustard
2 level tablespoons ground
ginger
4 drops Tabasco sauce

Hot, spicy and delicious with bread and cheese.

Measure the apple, onion, salt, vinegar, sugar and garlic into a microproof bowl and mix well. Cook on **full power** for 15 minutes, stirring twice during cooking, until the mixture is thick and pulpy. Reduce to a purée in a processor or blender and return to the bowl. Stir in the sultanas.

Blend the mustard, ginger and Tabasco together with a little of the chutney mixture until smooth, then stir into the chutney and mix well. Cook on **full power** for 10 minutes, then allow to cool. Leave to stand overnight until the sultanas have absorbed the excess liquid, then spoon into clean dry jars. Cover and label.

EASY FOOLPROOF MARMALADE

Power Level: Full
Cooking Time: About 40 Minutes per batch
Makes just over 6lb (2.75g)

1 thin-skinned juicy lemon
leftover peel of about 6
  satsumas
4lb (1.75kg) sugar

1 can prepared Seville
  oranges
about ¾ pint (450ml) water

This is made from a can of prepared, sliced Seville oranges with added lemons and satsuma skins – a very good way of using up skins that would normally just be thrown away. If you are making this in summer, use sweet oranges instead of satsumas. It is easiest to do the final boiling in two batches – this speeds up the process.

Peel the skin from the lemon thinly with a potato peeler and squeeze out the juice. Slice the peel from the lemon and satsumas into fine strips. Put into microproof glass measuring jug and pour over sufficient water to cover. Cover with pierced clear film and heat on **full power** for 8 minutes, or until the peel is tender.

Remove the peel with a slotted spoon and put into a large bowl with the sugar and the contents of the can. Add the lemon juice to the liquid in the jug and make up to ¾ pint (450ml) with water. Pour into the bowl with the fruit. Mix well together, then decant off half into another bowl.

Cook one of the bowls on **full power** for 3 minutes at a time, stirring in between until the sugar has dissolved (this will take about 15 minutes altogether), then return to the microwave for a further 15 minutes and test for setting point.

Put ½ teaspoon of the mixture on to a cold saucer and leave in the fridge for a few minutes then draw a finger over the surface of the marmalade. If it wrinkles then it is set; if not, boil for a further 2 minutes and retest.

Decant into clean dry jars. Cover, seal and label. Repeat process with the second batch.

LEMON CURD

Power Level: Full and Low   **Cooking Time:** 18–20 Minutes
Makes about 2lb (900g)

3 eggs	8oz (225g) granulated sugar
grated rind and juice of 3 large lemons	4oz (100g) butter

This is simple, easy and delicious when made in the microwave. Its keeping life is limited and so it should be prepared in small batches to ensure it is all used up quickly.

Measure the eggs and lemon rind into a large bowl and whisk well. Put the lemon juice, sugar and butter into a large microproof bowl and heat on **full power** for 5 minutes; stir until blended.

Whisking the eggs continuously, gradually pour in the melted butter mixture. Cook on **low power** for 13–15 minutes, stirring every few minutes to ensure none of the mixture overcooks, until the curd thickens and will coat the back of a spoon.

Spoon into clean dry jars, cover, seal and label. Keep in the refrigerator for up to 3 weeks.

Heating jams and jellies
Allow up to 1 minute on **full power**. The warmed jam spreads more easily on very fresh cakes.

Drink Up!

Have we time for that quick cuppa – or perhaps a glass of spicy mulled wine? They reheat in the microwave and taste freshly made! I often make a pot of coffee in advance, then reheat it to serve, piping hot, at the end of a meal. Just remember to leave enough room in the jug for the liquid to expand.

INSTANT COFFEE

The microwave is ideal for heating 1 or 2 cups of coffee, and for reheating ready-made coffee, either to serve at the end of a meal, or to reheat a cup that has been forgotten!

Measure the coffee into a cup, pour in cold water, leaving enough room for milk. Heat on **full power** for 2 to 2½ minutes until piping hot. Add milk and sugar to taste.

If making more than one cup, heat the coffee in a jug in the microwave, then pour into cups to serve.

THAT 'QUICK CUPPA'

Pour cold water into a cup or mug, heat on **full power** for 2 to 2½ minutes. Add a teabag and leave to infuse for the desired strength. Remove teabag and add sugar and milk to taste.

HOT WHISKY TODDY

Power Level: Full   **Cooking Time:** 2 Minutes
Serves 1

juice of 1 lemon
⅛ pint (65ml) water

1oz (25g) sugar
a good tot of whisky

Not guaranteed to cure a cold but it does help the patient feel better!

Measure the lemon juice, water and sugar into a strong glass. Heat on **full power** for 1 minute, stir until sugar dissolves. Return to the microwave and heat for a further 1 minute on **full power** until boiling. Stir in the whisky and serve.

MULLED WINE

Power Level: Full   **Cooking Time:** 11–12 Minutes
Serves 6

2 lemons
1 (70cl) bottle inexpensive
    red wine
1 pint (600ml) water
8 cloves

1 stick cinnamon
2–4oz (50–100g) caster sugar
4 tablespoons brandy or
    sherry
lemon slices, to decorate

A welcoming drink at a winter party

Thinly peel the zest from the lemons. Cut a few slices for decoration and leave on one side. Stand the remaining lemons, cut side down, in a glass bowl and heat on **full power** for 2 minutes. Squeeze out the juice.

Add the lemon zest, wine, water, cloves and cinnamon to the lemon juice in the bowl. Cover with pierced clear film and heat on **full power** for 5 minutes. Stir in sugar to taste and leave to stand until required. It's best to leave the wine for at least an hour to give the flavours time to develop.

To serve, remove the lemon zest, cloves and cinnamon and stir in the brandy or sherry. Reheat on **full power** for 4–5 minutes and serve hot with slices of lemon floating on the top.

Index

Index

Cooking for good health books – in paperback from Grafton Books

Pamela Westland

Low-Fat Cookery	£2.95	☐
Bean Feast	£2.50	☐
High-Fibre Vegetarian Cookery	£2.50	☐
The Complete Grill Cookbook	£1.50	☐

David Canter, Kay Canter and Daphne Swann

The Cranks Recipe Book (illustrated)	£3.95	☐

Cecilia Norman

Microwave Cookery for One	£2.50	☐
Microwave Cookery Course	£2.50	☐
The Pie and Pastry Cookbook	£2.50	☐
Barbecue Cookery	£1.95	☐
The Food Processor Cookbook	£1.95	☐

Mary Cadogan

Low-Salt Cookery	£1.95	☐

Colin Spencer

Colin Spencer's Vegetarian Wholefood Cookbook	£2.50	☐

To order direct from the publisher just tick the titles you want and fill in the order form. **HB481**

Cooking for good health books – in paperback from Grafton Books

Kenneth Lo

Cooking and Eating the Chinese Way	£1.95	☐
The Wok Cookbook	£1.95	☐
More Wok Cookery	£1.95	☐

L D Michaels

The Complete Book of Pressure Cooking	£1.95	☐

Franny Singer

The Slow Crock Cookbook	£1.95	☐

Janet Walker

Vegetarian Cookery	£2.50	☐

David Scott

The Japanese Cookbook	£1.95	☐

Marika Hanbury Tenison

Cooking with Vegetables (illustrated)	£1.95	☐
Deep-Freeze Cookery	£1.95	☐

Pamela Westland

Low-Fat Cookery	£2.95	☐
Bean Feast	£2.50	☐
High-Fibre Vegetarian Cookery	£2.50	☐
The Complete Grill Cookbook	£1.50	☐

David Canter, Kay Canter and Daphne Swann

The Cranks Recipe Book (illustrated)	£3.95	☐

To order direct from the publisher just tick the titles you want and fill in the order form.

HB381

International cookery books in paperback from
Grafton Books

Elizabeth Cass
Spanish Cooking   £1.25   ☐

Arto der Haroutunian
Complete Arab Cookery   £2.50   ☐
Modern Jewish Cookery   £2.50   ☐

Robin Howe
Greek Cooking   £1.95   ☐
German Cooking   £1.95   ☐
Italian Cooking   £1.95   ☐

Kenneth Lo
Cooking and Eating the Chinese Way   £1.95   ☐
The Wok Cookbook   £1.95   ☐
More Wok Cookery   £1.95   ☐

F Marian McNeil
The Scots Kitchen (illustrated)   £2.50   ☐
The Scots Cellar   £1.95   ☐

David Scott
The Japanese Cookbook   £1.95   ☐

E P Veerasawmy
Indian Cookery   £2.50   ☐

Kenneth Gardnier
Creole Caribbean Cookery   £3.95   ☐

To order direct from the publisher just tick the titles you want
and fill in the order form.   **HB581**

Cookery handbooks now available in paperback from Grafton Books

L D Michaels
The Complete Book of Pressure Cooking £1.95 ☐

Cecilia Norman
Microwave Cookery for One £2.50 ☐
Microwave Cookery Course £2.50 ☐
The Pie and Pastry Cookbook £2.50 ☐
Barbecue Cookery £1.95 ☐
The Food Processor Cookbook £1.95 ☐

Franny Singer
The Slow Crock Cookbook £1.95 ☐

Janet Walker
Vegetarian Cookery £2.50 ☐

Pamela Westland
Low-Fat Cookery £2.95 ☐
Bean Feast £2.50 ☐
High-Fibre Vegetarian Cookery £2.50 ☐
The Complete Grill Cookbook £1.50 ☐

Marika Hanbury Tenison
Deep-Freeze Cookery £1.95 ☐
Cooking with Vegetables (illustrated) £1.95 ☐

Jennifer Stone
The Alcoholic Cookbook £1.95 ☐

Barbara Griggs
Baby's Cookbook £1.95 ☐

Wendy Craig
Busy Mum's Cookbook £1.95 ☐

Carolyn Heal and Michael Allsop
Cooking with Spices £2.95 ☐

To order direct from the publisher just tick the titles you want
and fill in the order form.

HB681

Gardening books now available in paperback from Grafton Books

Roy Genders (Editor)

Pears Encyclopaedia of Gardening	£0.00	☐
Fruit and Vegetables	£1.25	☐
Flowers, Trees and Shrubs	£2.50	☐

Shirley Ross

First Aid for Houseplants	£1.95	☐

HB781

Health and self-help books – in paperback from Grafton Books

W H Bates		
Better Eyesight Without Glasses	£2.50	☐
Laurence E Morehouse and Leonard Gross		
Total Fitness	£2.50	☐
Constance Mellor		
Guide to Natural Health	£1.25	☐
Natural Remedies for Common Ailments	£1.95	☐
Sonya Richmond		
Yoga and Your Health	£1.25	☐
Phyllis Speight		
Homoeopathy	£1.50	☐
Dr Richard B Stuart		
Act Thin, Stay Thin	£1.50	☐
Dr Carl C Pfeiffer and Jane Banks		
Total Nutrition	£1.50	☐
Dr Hamilton Hall		
Be Your Own Back Doctor	£2.50	☐
José Silva and Michael Miele		
The Silva Mind Control Method	£2.95	☐
Geneen Roth		
Breaking Free from Compulsive Eating	£2.95	☐
Feeding the Hungry Heart	£2.50	☐

Titles of General Interest – in paperback from Grafton Books

Malcolm MacPherson (Editor)
The Black Box: Cockpit Voice Recorder
Accounts of Nineteen Air Accidents   £1.95 ☐

Isaac Asimov
Asimov on Science Fiction   £2.50 ☐

Roy Harley Lewis
The Browser's Guide to Erotica   £1.95 ☐

Charles Berlitz
Native Tongues   £2.50 ☐

Carole Boyer
Names for Boys and Girls   £1.95 ☐

José Silva and Michael Miele
The Silva Mind Control Method   £2.95 ☐

Millard Arnold (Editor)
The Testimony of Steve Biko   £2.50 ☐

John Howard Griffin
Black Like Me   £1.95 ☐

Desmond Morris
The Naked Ape   £2.95 ☐
The Pocket Guide to Man Watching (illustrated)   £5.95 ☐

Ivan Tyrell
The Survival Option   £2.50 ☐

Peter Laurie
Beneath the City Streets   £2.50 ☐

To order direct from the publisher just tick the titles you want
and fill in the order form.   **HB1082**

All these books are available at your local bookshop or newsagent, or can be ordered direct from the publisher.

To order direct from the publishers just tick the titles you want and fill in the form below.

Name _____

Address _____

_____

Send to:
Grafton Cash Sales
PO Box 11, Falmouth, Cornwall TR10 9EN.

Please enclose remittance to the value of the cover price plus:

UK 60p for the first book, 25p for the second book plus 15p per copy for each additional book ordered to a maximum charge of £1.90.

BFPO 60p for the first book, 25p for the second book plus 15p per copy for the next 7 books, thereafter 9p per book.

Overseas including Eire £1.25 for the first book, 75p for second book and 28p for each additional book.

Grafton Books reserve the right to show new retail prices on covers, which may differ from those previously advertised in the text or elsewhere.

STAR WARS®

THE CLONE WARS™

DEFENDERS OF THE LOST TEMPLE

DESIGNER **KRYSTAL HENNES**

ASSISTANT EDITOR **FREDDYE LINS**

EDITOR **DAVE MARSHALL**

PUBLISHER **MIKE RICHARDSON**

Special thanks to Joanne Chan Taylor, Leland Chee, Troy Alders, Carol Roeder, Jann Moorhead, and David Anderman at Lucas Licensing.

Published by Dark Horse Books, a division of Dark Horse Comics, Inc.
10956 SE Main Street, Milwaukie, OR 97222

DarkHorse.com | StarWars.com

To find a comics shop in your area, call the Comic Shop Locator Service toll-free at 1.888.266.4226
First edition: March 2013 | ISBN 978-1-61655-058-5

10 9 8 7 6 5 4 3 2 1

Printed in China

Library of Congress Cataloging-in-Publication Data

Aclin, Justin.
Star Wars, the clone wars. Defenders of the lost temple / script, Justin Aclin ; art, Ben Bates ; colors, Michael Atiyeh ; lettering, Michael Heisler ; cover art, Mike Hawthorne. -- 1st ed.
    p. cm.
Summary: On a mission with a Jedi general, one clone trooper discovers who he is and where he came from when a group of the warrior Mandalorians appear.
ISBN 978-1-61655-058-5
1. Star Wars fiction. 2. Extraterrestrial beings--Comic books, strips, etc. 3. Extraterrestrial beings--Juvenile fiction. 4. Space warfare--Comic books, strips, etc. 5. Space warfare--Juvenile fiction. 6. Graphic novels. [1. Graphic novels. 2. Extraterrestrial beings--Fiction. 3. Space warfare--Fiction.] I. Bates, Ben, 1982- ill. II. Hawthorne, Mike, ill. III. Title. IV. Title: Defenders of the lost temple.
PZ7.7.A28Sth 2013
741.5'973--dc23

                        2012040395

STAR WARS: THE CLONE WARS—DEFENDERS OF THE LOST TEMPLE

STAR WARS®

THE CLONE WARS™

DEFENDERS OF THE LOST TEMPLE

SCRIPT **JUSTIN ACLIN**   ART **BEN BATES**

COLORS **MICHAEL ATIYEH**   LETTERING **MICHAEL HEISLER**

COVER ART **MIKE HAWTHORNE**

DARK HORSE BOOKS

LUCAS BOOKS

This story takes place sometime between seasons 4 and 5 of *The Clone Wars*.

ACCORDING TO THE HOLOCRON, THE TEMPLE SHOULD BE JUST OVER THE TOP OF THIS...

...HILL.

LOOKS LIKE THE HOLOCRON WAS RIGHT.

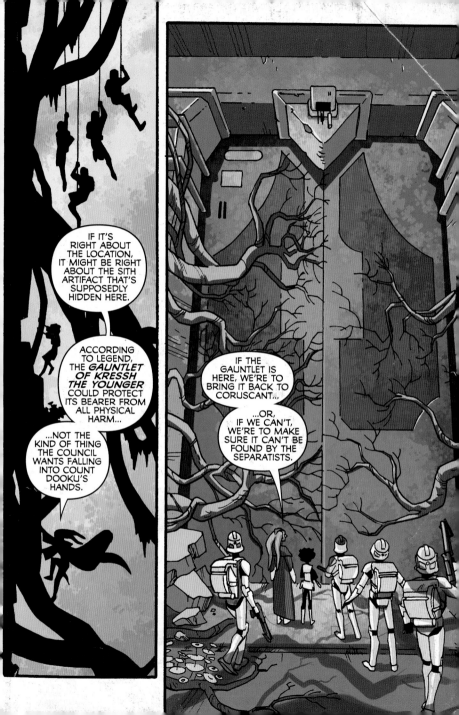

HORNS, I'VE GOT TO ASK YOU...

WHAT'S THE STORY WITH YOUR HELMET?

THIS?

THAT'S THE SYMBOL OF THE *MANDALORIAN DEATH WATCH.*

I KNOW THAT -- BUT DEATH WATCH ARE MANIACS.

WHY HAVE THEIR SYMBOL ON YOUR HELMET?

DEATH WATCH ARE THE MOST DANGEROUS MANDALORIAN WARRIORS IN THE GALAXY...

AND I'M ONE OF THE DEADLIEST CLONES OF A GREAT MANDALORIAN WARRIOR!

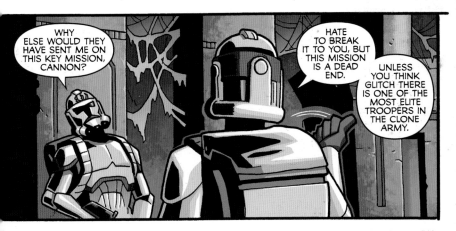

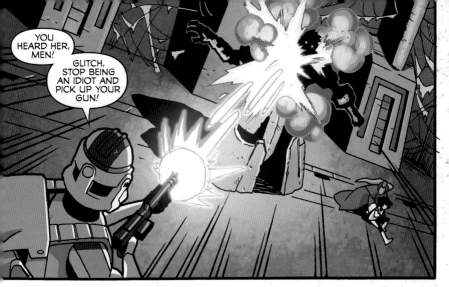

USE THE FORCE... BUT NOT TO ATTACK!

CLICK CLICK CLICK CLICK

CLICK

UH, GUYS...

HAVE WE -- *OOF* -- FIGURED OUT HOW TO STOP THESE THINGS YET?

THANK THE FORCE!

WRONG PLACE AT THE WRONG TIME AGAIN, GLITCH?

SARLS!

RENNAX, HELP ME FREE THE TROOPERS -- I'LL GO FOR THE GAUNTLET!

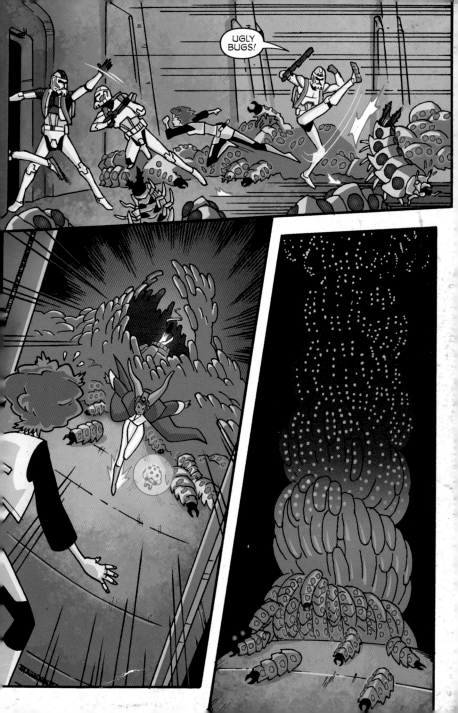

WE'LL MAKE CAMP HERE FOR THE NIGHT.

I'LL CONTACT THE COUNCIL ON CORUSCANT IN THE MORNING...MAYBE THEY'LL KNOW WHAT TO DO.

I'LL SEAL THE CHAMBER.

VSSH

RRRR RRUMBLE

THERE!

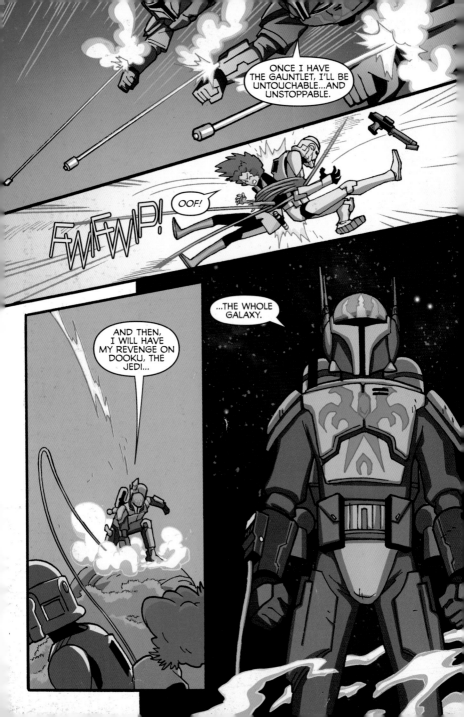

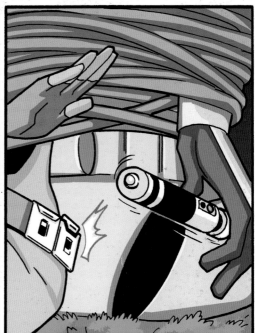

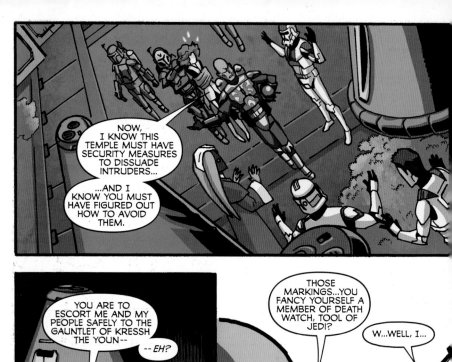

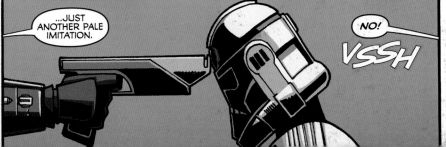

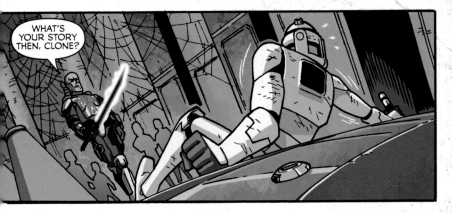

THANK YOU, TROOPER GLITCH.

SO LONG, GLITCH. YOU WERE A TERRIBLE CLONE TROOPER...

...BUT YOU WERE A GREAT MAN.

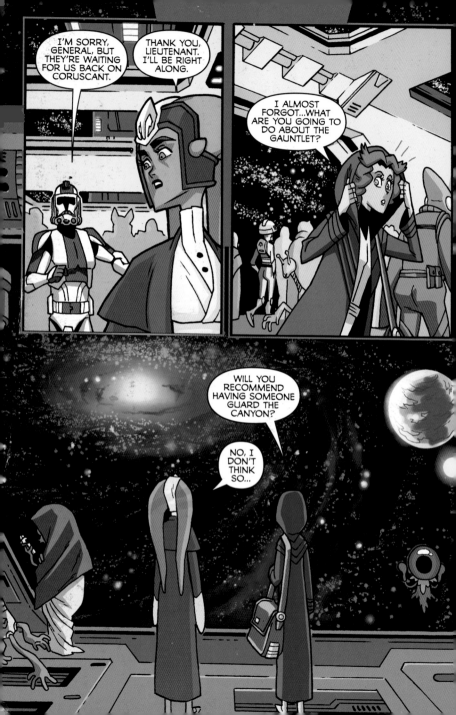

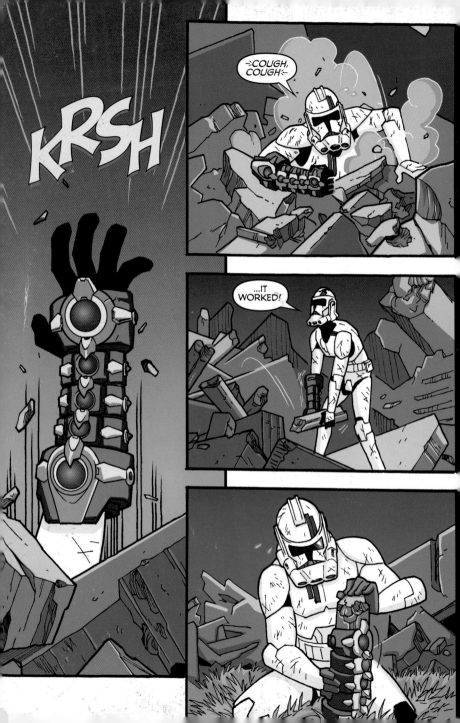

STAR WARS GRAPHIC NOVEL TIMELINE (IN YEARS)

Omnibus: Tales of the Jedi—5,000–3,986 BSW4

Knights of the Old Republic—3,964–3,963 BSW4

The Old Republic—3653, 3678 BSW4

Knight Errant—1,032 BSW4

Jedi vs. Sith—1,000 BSW4

Omnibus: Rise of the Sith—33 BSW4

Episode I: The Phantom Menace—32 BSW4

Omnibus: Emissaries and Assassins—32 BSW4

Omnibus: Quinlan Vos—Jedi in Darkness—31–30 BSW4

Omnibus: Menace Revealed—31–22 BSW4

Honor and Duty—22 BSW4

Blood Ties—22 BSW4

Episode II: Attack of the Clones—22 BSW4

Clone Wars—22–19 BSW4

Clone Wars Adventures—22–19 BSW4

General Grievous—22–19 BSW4

Episode III: Revenge of the Sith—19 BSW4

Dark Times—19 BSW4

Omnibus: Droids—5.5 BSW4

Omnibus: Boba Fett—3 BSW4–10 ASW4

Omnibus: At War with the Empire—1 BSW4

Episode IV: A New Hope—SW4

Classic Star Wars—0–3 ASW4

Omnibus: A Long Time Ago . . .—0–4 ASW4

Empire—0 ASW4

Omnibus: The Other Sons of Tatooine—0 ASW4

Omnibus: Early Victories—0–3 ASW4

Jabba the Hutt: The Art of the Deal—1 ASW4

Episode V: The Empire Strikes Back—3 ASW4

Omnibus: Shadows of the Empire—3.5–4.5 ASW4

Episode VI: Return of the Jedi—4 ASW4

Omnibus: X-Wing Rogue Squadron—4–5 ASW4

Heir to the Empire—9 ASW4

Dark Force Rising—9 ASW4

The Last Command—9 ASW4

Dark Empire—10 ASW4

Crimson Empire—11 ASW4

Jedi Academy: Leviathan—12 ASW4

Union—19 ASW4

Chewbacca—25 ASW4

Invasion—25 ASW4

Legacy—130–137 ASW4

Old Republic Era
25,000 – 1000 years before
Star Wars: A New Hope

Rise of the Empire Era
1000 – 0 years before
Star Wars: A New Hope

Rebellion Era
0 – 5 years after
Star Wars: A New Hope

New Republic Era
5 – 25 years after
Star Wars: A New Hope

New Jedi Order Era
25+ years after
Star Wars: A New Hope

Legacy Era
130+ years after
Star Wars: A New Hope

Infinities
Does not apply to timeline

Sergio Aragones Stomps Star Wars
Star Wars Tales
Infinities
Tag and Bink
Star Wars Visionaries

BSW4 = before *Episode IV: A New Hope*. ASW4 = after *Episode IV: A New Hope*.

FOR MORE ADVENTURE IN A GALAXY FAR, FAR, AWAY...

**STAR WARS: THE CLONE WARS—
THE WIND RAIDERS OF TALORAAN**
978-1-59582-231-4 | $7.99

**STAR WARS ADVENTURES:
LUKE SKYWALKER AND THE
TREASURE OF THE DRAGONSNAKES**
978-1-59582-347-2 | $7.99

STAR WARS®

CLONE WARS ADVENTURES

Don't miss any of the action-packed adventures of your favorite **STAR WARS**® characters, available at comics shops and bookstores in a galaxy near you!

$6.99 each!

Volume 1	Volume 2	Volume 3	Volume 4	Volume 5
ISBN 978-1-59307-243-8	ISBN 978-1-59307-271-1	ISBN 978-1-59307-307-7	ISBN 978-1-59307-402-9	ISBN 978-1-59307-483-8
Volume 6	Volume 7	Volume 8	Volume 9	Volume 10
ISBN 978-1-59307-567-5	ISBN 978-1-59307-678-8	ISBN 978-1-59307-680-1	ISBN 978-1-59307-832-4	ISBN 978-1-59307-878-2